50

thorns & blossoms

julie marie todd

50: thorns & blossoms

Copyright © 2019 by Julie Marie Todd

In Medias Res, LLC
1009 Quincy Street
Onalaska, WI 54650

ISBN 978-0-9911005-7-6

Library of Congress Control Number:2019909520

Acknowledgments / Thank You to:

Reflections: Narratives of Professional Helping for permission to reprint
"Confessions of a Christian Supremacist"

Desert Call: Contemplative Spirituality and Vital Culture for permission to
reprint "Spirituality and Service," originally titled, "A Ridiculous
Frivolity"

Rain and Thunder: A Radical Feminist Journal of Discussion and Activism
for permission to reprint "THIS CREASE IN MY BROW"

Haven Herrin for the cover design and internal graphics.
Illustrations © 2019 by Haven Herrin

Todd, Julie Marie 1968–
50: thorns & blossoms / Julie Marie Todd
1. BODY, MIND & SPIRIT / General
2. POETRY / Subjects & Themes / Inspirational & Religious
3. RELIGION / Christian Living / General

Table of Contents

Introduction & Acknowledgments i

Single & Celibate: How Masturbation Saved My Life.........................1

Grief Pensée..13

Power & Persuasion...21

My Soul Is Tom Brady 27

DUMB BITCH 33

Public Resurrection 43

Confessions of a Christian Supremacist 53

Healthy Boundaries (On containment) 65

ANIMAL BODIES (with all my love to Eli) 69

Ordination Day (I Shit Myself) 75

The Deer 87

Spirituality and Service..93

THIS CREASE IN MY BROW...99

Offering My Heart to God 103

I am oatstraw 105

Cultivating (Sativa) Desire..109

A Letter from and to My Body...113

Nothing Left to Give (In Memory of Webb) 117

You Can't Put Constraints On the Soul 121

RED BELL BOTTOM JEANS..125

Psalm 51 Rewrite 129

Ode to SNIRT 133

The Foolishness of Love...137

Do I Have a Poem In Me Today? 139

I dare you 141

Vulnerability...145

Still Can't Fucking Write..149

If I became blind..153

What Makes Me Weary? 155

The Need to Breathe (I CAN'T BREATHE, HE SAID) 159

On Church Unity...165

Fearfully Wonderfully..169

How Queer 171

The High of Being Mighty...173

Influence 179

DONE WITH TOXIC BULLSHIT (on my parasite cleanse).........183

Lies & Apple Pies 187

Little Toes (bunion surgery sucks).......................................191

The Thing [I Thought] I Was Most Afraid to Write About 193

goodbye, motherhood...197

I Will Not Join the What The Fuck Army of One 199

From the Hectic to the Slow Filling of Days........................205

The People's Grocery & the Lynching at the Curve 207

Full Moon Jesus 217

An Existence Hewn of Rock...225

Thank you, church...227

UnEarthing The Understory (homage to Lily of the Valley)...........229

no imposter..233

Dust of Stars 235

When Spires Fall (Who Are We?) 241

About Julie..249

Introduction & Acknowledgments

In 2018 I turned 50. This book is a selection of 50 things I have written since 2007, when a significant period of writing began in my life. Though I have included a few lengthier prose essays and previously published works, most of what I offer here is what I call poetic prose, predominantly long-form, stream-of-consciousness writing.

Most of these pieces were written by hand in journals, both personal journal entries as well as journals used in writing groups. I have put them in chronological order as they were dated. The longer essays are the most significantly edited. Though I edited others in the process of transcription and formatting, I tried to maintain the manner in which poems fell out of my pen and onto the paper, keeping the indentation, capitalization, punctuation, underlining, and sentence or phrase line-length intact. When something comes out of me of this nature, it comes out fairly whole. Where I think that a bit of context might aid in understanding, I have added a postscript in italics.

These are personal pieces. I share them as parts of who I have been, who I am, how I feel, what I think, and who I am becoming. While the content may seem like a revelation to some, their release in this form feels like a closing of a chapter, an honoring and expression of my life.

Mom and Dad, Mary and Jim Todd, there are no adequate words to express my love to you and for you. You have never failed to love and support me in any decision of my life or expression of my self, ever. Thank you.

Rania Henriquez and Celeste Cruz, thank you. Our conversation in my apartment on Kent Street was the precipitating factor in my decision to compile these writings. You will forever be my favorite writers.

To the members of the Guerrilla Society, The Common Sage adult writing group, and all descendants of the Andover Bread Loaf network in Lawrence, MA: thank you. The acts of writing and sharing with you regularly inspired me daily, blew my mind, caused me to grow and change, think, create community and become vulnerable in ways that I had not envisioned. What a pleasure and honor it has been to write with you all. Through you, my authentic writing voice emerged. Thank you for helping me know my words are worthy to be shared, no disclaimers.

Deep gratitude for three of my comrades from Love Prevails: Wesley White and Brenda Smith White for helping me edit, format, and publish, and Haven Herrin for the amazing book cover and graphics. This book would neither be in existence nor look as fine as it does without them. Love Prevails' actions of collective resistance against LGBTQ+ exclusion and discrimination in The United Methodist Church were some of the terrain in which I also discovered, honed, and found encouragement for my writing voice. Our collective acts of written critical analysis proved to me the power of combining direct action with alternative, public narratives in the shaping of social transformation.

Julie Marie Todd
October 2019
Lawrence, MA

Single & Celibate:
How Masturbation Saved My Life

Lying around one post-sex sunny afternoon, my boyfriend of a few weeks asked me, "So, do you wonk?"

I thought, "Wonk? Does that mean fuck?" It couldn't mean fuck since the answer was patently obvious. "Wonk?" I asked.

He responded, "That's not American English?" I had recently met this guy in the city where I was living in another country. His first English teacher outside of a high school classroom was his previous English-speaking girlfriend he met while living in Canada, who I think was actually from the UK, or maybe Australia – whichever country uses the word 'wonk.' He said, "It means, you know, make yourself have a – orgasm?"

"Ooohhh," I said. "You mean masturbate." We launched into an American English language lesson for slang words for masturbation – getting off, jacking off, and so on. I explained that American men had numerous unfortunate phrases. The first one that I remember learning was "choke the chicken."(High school church camp.)

The English lesson provided enough diversion from his original question about wonking to give me a chance to consider my answer. When he asked again, "So, do you?" I was fully prepared to lie. "Sure," I said, "doesn't everyone?" Then he asked me to get off in front of him and I said something about it being a private thing, and why did I need to when I had him? Both of us feeling good about the latter response, that was the end of the topic.

The plain truth was that not only had I never wonked, I can't say I had even talked about it, perhaps even thought about it to any degree. Since at the tender age of 24, this guy was the first really good lover I had and the first to treat me to a full-on orgasm, I really hadn't known what I was missing.

I am sure that masturbation was mentioned in the book on women's bodies that my mom gave me when I was a tweenager. But I was so mortified that my mother was attempting to communicate with me about sex, I do not remember anything about the book but that she gave it to me and that it had pictures of women's body parts. She was, I'm sure, trying earnestly to own her feminism and break the silence of her own moralistic, southern Methodist upbringing. She did not force a conversation about sexual behavior with me. There weren't any kind of "nice girls don't do it" or moralistic Christian expressions against sexual behavior that I can remember.

Any conversation I remember about masturbation made it appear to be behavior for boys, and pathetic boys at that. I can remember hearing the language of "wet dreams" and "cumming," along with choking the chicken. But the most I could gather was that if you were a Catholic boy and you did it you were going to hell. The Catholics always seemed to have it bad.

The first public conversation that I had about sex at all was at high school church camp. The camp counselor ripped open a condom package, and I saw my first condom unwrapped. Another explained that the term "scumbag" referred to the tip of the condom where the semen gathers after ejaculation, a process which was also described. Fascinating. Pretty shocking and revolutionary for church camp. But, while remarkable, now I realize that the conversation about sex education was deeply flawed. It implied that the sexual pleasuring was only meant to be between two people, and those two people would necessarily be a man and a woman. To support the important promotion of safe sex, it made no mention that a condom was an unnecessary device for women if their goal was orgasm. No mention of do-it-yourself; no mention of intimate relations other than heterosexual. Thinking back, what seemed so earthshaking for church camp was not entirely out of the box, but I thank God that those counselors had the balls to talk about it at all.

But even their silence on DIY serves to reinforce my main point in this whole business: for women, the masturbation thing was totally under wraps in my WASP (White, Anglo-Saxon, Protestant) Yankee world. It wasn't some explicit creepy chastity and purity bullshit indoctrination. In my mind now, the silence was part of an outright conspiracy to deny women their power. And it still is. But back to my boyfriend.

When I met him, I was three months shy of finishing a two-year stint as a foreign missionary for my denomination. I know, I know; not a very missionary position. My young lover followed me home to the U.S. and we spent a lovely summer together that ended in a situation of no-job-no-visa unrequited love. At the end of the summer, we arranged for him to leave flying out of Washington, D.C., where I rendezvoused with an American girlfriend I knew from our teaching abroad. She was leading a group of college students on a summer exchange. The night boyfriend and I bid adieu, girlfriend and I hit a club with one of her colleagues. While the bass pounded, we sat in a big booth drowning my sadness in alcohol. She asked me about the future – would he and I attempt a long-distance relationship? I said we would. This girlfriend understood. Her husband had work that took him away from home for 2 to 3 months at a time.

I asked, "How do you do it?"

She answered, "All I can say is, thank God for masturbation."

There it was again. I was completely stunned. Fortunately, we had another language lesson diversion to explain to her colleague what masturbation was. This led to some great laughs and I played along describing masturbation like I knew what the hell I was talking about. Apparently, not only did my friend masturbate but she was also willing to talk about it. I might also mention that she was Roman

Catholic. I, still, could only pretend. But the concept was emblazoned in my mind. I was on a mission to masturbate.

I bought a book in the D.C. airport: *For Yourself: The Fulfillment of Female Sexuality* by Lonnie Garfield Barbach (Garden City, NY: Doubleday and Co., 1975). Published originally in the mid-seventies, now I understand it to be stock-in-trade women-get-to-know-your-bodies material. But what I learned then was that many, many women had never had orgasms. To my amazement, this was as true for partnered people as single people. This made me feel particularly bad for partnered women not only because so many were in crappy relationships with assholes or pathetic, boring men (so many, so sad), but could not even console themselves with the fact that at least they were having orgasms (doubly sad). But the main thing I connected with was that the biggest problem was that so few women could and would even talk about it.

Barbach described some pointers for getting to orgasm yourself. Get to know your genital parts with a mirror. Feel them, stick your fingers in them, move them around. Notice the colors. The textures. The sensations. She called it a fact-finding mission. As important, she explained the notion that in this phallocentric world, women are taught to believe that orgasm comes primarily through vaginal penetration. That is why traditional sexual intercourse leaves women feeling so confused because they think they are supposed to have an orgasm that way. When we don't, then we think that something is wrong with us. What women don't realize is that vaginal intercourse often does not provoke enough direct stimulation of the clitoris, which is the primary genital area for orgasmic pleasure because of its density of nerve endings. Whether we want to have sex with another person or not, Barbach counsels, if we want to know how it works for maximum pleasure, we need to find out for ourselves.

The boyfriend gone, it is late summer, and I am armed for the revolution with my book. It is one of those horrible hot and humid days when you don't want to move for fear of profusely sweating. Looked at my outside genital parts in the mirror on the toilet. Then I got on top of the covers. Fan blowing on my naked body. Barbach said sometimes it takes time to figure out where you gotta go to get it to feel good. Some women need a hard rub. Some like it soft. Be patient, she wrote, and you will surely figure it out. If you need some help getting excited, fantasize; and don't judge what comes to mind. It is going to start to feel good, feel better, feel great. Touch other parts of your body. Contract your muscles. Release. You are going to realize, through your own increasing response, you are eventually going to give yourself an orgasm. "So let me repeat: consistent, continuous stimulation of a type dictated by individual preference is required to bring a woman to orgasm." For some women, it takes a long time to orgasm. For some women it takes a short time. Sometimes one, sometimes more than one. The same woman may be different every time. Learn to enjoy satisfying yourself.

I had a tall pink Tupperware plastic tumbler filled with warm water because the idea of using cooking oil on my vagina freaked me right out. She described what it might start feeling like down there that may be different than when you are having sex with someone else. For me, it didn't take long. It didn't take a fantasy. It was brief, and it worked. I could not believe I had denied myself this pleasure until now. Maybe it was the next day; I tried the removable massage showerhead. The revolution was on.

This was the end of the summer immediately before my first year in seminary. I am not joking when I say I took on a power that I did not know I had. I was so much more in myself, growing into a knowledge of my own body and the power of it, and I loved it. I felt I had some control over myself for the first time in my life.

At the same time, I was entering into a world of academia where in myriad ways I would be told that I did not know what I believed that I knew and that knowledge of myself and what I desired to know was not adequate. Of course, there were levels at which this was entirely true. There was very much that I did not know or understand about the content of courses, about myself, about church and community ministry, particularly in relation to questions of power and privilege.

But there were some things that I was certain that I understood were deeply wrong with the process and content of my education in seminary. I was shocked to be in a liberal seminary in the mid-nineties to confront a curriculum without any significant content geared to women or people of color, a faculty with no tenured women of any race, syllabi with an almost complete exclusion of marginalized voices, and learning and worship settings that did not demand the use of inclusive language for God and humanity. Later I was to learn that I was at the seminary at a time only a few years removed from a virtual feminist and lesbian witch-hunt. Every attempt that I and others made to confront these systems of male domination was met with resounding opposition from students, faculty, and administration. I was accused at every turn of not knowing what I was talking about.

During my three years of seminary, the debates about sexual orientation in Protestant denominations were becoming central. Pro-LGBTQ denominational bodies were gathering steam to fight the growing anti-queer policies and behaviors of conservative movements. In my own denomination we were signing up "Reconciling United Methodists" for the 1996 General Conference, and there was freakish fear among straight people in seminaries about signing up and being labeled as gay or pro-gay in their annual conferences and ordaining bodies. Straight candidates for ministry were afraid that they would be denied ordination for allying with gay people. They likened their potential persecution and marginalization for supporting gay people to the actual exclusion of gay people from the church itself, as if they had a clue.

The only people I personally knew at this point in my life who ever had to answer any questions whatsoever from their committees or boards of ordained ministry about matters related to sexuality were single women who appeared or were known to be heterosexual. These committees never asked these women if they were lesbians, or if they were going to marry gay people against our denomination's policy. They asked them if they were going to be able to abstain from sex as single clergywomen; whether, once ordained, they would be able to uphold the highest Christian ideal of "celibacy in singleness."

This "fidelity in marriage and celibacy in singleness" language is a key to the exclusion of gay and lesbian persons from ordination. In my denomination "self-avowed, practicing homosexuals" are not permitted to be ordained. At the time these rules were created, there were no legal state same-gender unions or marriages, so gay men and lesbians in same-gender partnerships would be neither technically married nor celibate. In my neck of the woods, boards of ministry began asking the question about celibacy to persons well-known to be heterosexual to demonstrate that they were being "fair" about "applying the law" to everyone. But the problem with this "fair application of the law" is that the only people who were ever asked about their sexual behavior during the course of their ordination process were single women. And it was always along the lines of whether or not they could "handle" not having sex if they had a boyfriend or were engaged. I do not know of a single, single man who was subjected to this line of questioning, nor married people who were ever asked if they could "handle" being faithful.

This double-triple standard and hypocritical reasoning makes plain that the language of single and celibate is not expressive of an ideal about holy living, but is a means of policing sexual behavior on the part of parties who are deemed by the patriarchy to represent the greatest threat to male power: people who might potentially deviate from married, heterosexual behavior. The church's policies around sexual behavior help to maintain the heteropatriarchy so that the marginalized do not know the power they have to subvert the dominant paradigm through other forms of social organization.

That is part of the reason why masturbation saved my life. By the time I am into and out of seminary, I am in full control of my own sexual power, and no one is going to take it from me. And for that matter, no one is going to take it from anyone else if I have anything to say about it. In my ordination process, I had decided that if they asked me about my singleness and celibacy, I was going to tell them, "My dad (also a pastor in the region) told me to masturbate." I figured that would shut them up. Or else I would just tell them to go fuck themselves. Or I would institute a ritual at our regional annual meeting in which every ordinand was publicly questioned about their sexual behavior. Oh, I had lots of ideas. Of course, they never asked me.

When I was finally ordained, when they asked me if I would uphold "the highest ideals of Christian living," and our *Book of Discipline* (including the mandates not to marry gay people and so on),

I swear to God I crossed my fingers behind my back while I lied like a five-year old. In seminary, I had heard Virginia Ramey Mollenkott give a lecture on "Ethics in a War Zone." She said that like soldiers who understand that there is a different code of ethics during wartime, women and gay people in the heteropatriarchy of the church live in a war zone and were thus sanctioned to lie to protect ourselves and fight the war. So in the biblical tradition of Shiprah and Puah, I lied, and I really feel that God was good with that then and still is.

Because I, and not the church, was in control of my sexual power, I was never afraid of what people thought about me and my sexuality. Over the course of years of local church service, I invited people, men and women, to live in the parsonage with me many times. Nobody ever knew if I was partnered with these people or not. I considered it none of their business. My body, my power, my home, period. I was an open advocate of the pro-LGBTQ movement. So some people assumed I must be a lesbian. I was "accused" of being a lesbian by a parishioner. I was coveted as a lesbian. Why would a straight person be so passionately committed to such work? You wonder if I'm queer? Ask me. Then, fuck you, because you know what? It's none of your business. To this day, most of my colleagues and parishioners have no idea what my sexual orientation is. And I like it that way. It is none of anyone's damn business.

In reality, I didn't have a lot of partners. Like many other single women in ministry, I burned myself out and down to the ground a number of times with workaholic behavior, found it difficult to meet people, and was afraid to date in the community anyway. When I did date, I was exceedingly private about it, and those relationships were exceedingly partial. Masturbation saw me through some very dry times, thank God. But it didn't substitute for human contact. When I had sex, having come to know my body through masturbation, the pleasure of my partnered sex life expanded. I had learned about my sexual responsiveness on my own and was increasingly able to communicate to meet my needs. And I felt I had legitimately lied about being celibate. Anyway, if someone "found out" I was having sex, what were they going to do, put me on trial? I actually coveted the idea of the church putting all of the people I was ever suspected of having a relationship with on the stand and asking them if we had ever had genital contact. And never finding out if, or with whom, I did. I joke about these things with the full realization, however, that faithful ministers in my denomination have been put on trial for assumed same-sex genital contact, and this is no joke. It is painful and humiliating, and admitting my fantasy trial is only to demonstrate how foolish, destructive, and awful the whole thing is.

I do not wish that the picture I am painting of myself covers up an admission that, like many pastors, especially women, I was an extreme people-pleaser. It wasn't as if I was walking around my church telling people to go fuck themselves all the time. What I am trying to express is that masturbation gave me the first inkling of what it meant to also please myself, also to care for myself, to have authority over myself, and to love my own body. This self-knowledge was crucial in the midst of a profession with intense pressures to please and perform, and within a tradition that denies the goodness of the body and its pleasures. These pressures seriously throw one's own sense of self into question. This is particularly true in a church and society which tell you not to be partnered means not to be whole.

The picture I do wish to paint is that the attitude of stridency encouraged by my masturbating extended into my politics in the church and elsewhere. When you realize that you have this power of body and mind, that people can't fuck with you literally unless you let them, or you want them to, there is an important aspect to this knowing yourself to be fully possessed by yourself and God, that, frankly, I've found to be pretty powerful in the work of pastoring and politicking in the church. I realize that this individual sense of power is reinforced by the privileges of race and class and lifelong Christian privilege that I also bring to the community table. But my prophetic commitment to undoing these systems of privilege requires a certain internal sense of body-mind presence that cannot be undone by the systems of domination that will try to ruin you if you are really doing the work. Masturbation has helped instill in me a body-mind presence that has been critical in preserving my life and spirit in the midst of anti-oppression work.

I also recognize that there are oodles of masturbating women who are chicken-shit when it comes to politics. Masturbation does not always translate to a sense of personal presence or power in prophetic speech and action. To you women, I say, take the power you have over your own masturbating body and channel it with whatever other privilege you have to make a difference in the world, for God's sake. At the very least you should know that if you fail, you can be sure that you still have yourself to please.

And as far as my spiritual life goes, what more obvious sign is there that God is with me than masturbation? This may sound tongue and cheek, but I am serious about this. My church's stance on sexuality says that it is a good gift of God. The clitoris. I mean, if this isn't a marvelous creative gift of the good God, what is? A gift that serves no other purpose than pleasuring? Only for women? What masturbation has done for my theology of embodiment and spiritual connection with God, I can hardly begin to describe. God gave me this beautiful thing as a part of my learning to love myself as God loves me, every part of me. I am starting to think God gave us the clitoris for the express purpose of surviving the patriarchy.

Since becoming ordained, one primary aspect of my spiritual journey has been about learning to be less rigid with myself and others, more compassionate. In other words, in the midst of living out a serious spiritual vocation, I seriously need to lighten the fuck up. I literally cannot imagine what all the years of seminary and ministry would have been like if I had not masturbated. If I had had to keep all of that energy of anger and sadness and anxiety and pressure pent up, my head might have blown right off of my shoulders. I wonder if, without masturbation, I wouldn't have been the worst kind of self-destruction machine. I swear I would be miserable. You thought I was joking when I said it saved my life. Masturbation is one way I have taught myself to enjoy myself. In the midst of non-stop work life, to take a break and focus only on myself. In the kind of work that demands so much thinking, to be in touch with my emotions and sensations in my body. In the harsh reality of striving for justice, to live in a fantasy world for a while. In a world of pent-up emotion, to release, to let go. I thank God for it.

I also thank God that it has helped me to stay single. It has helped to prevent me from careening any further into relationships that I might have made a premature commitment to for the sake of some bullshit cultural pair-bonding norm that the vast majority of women buy into. For me, it isn't about being celibate, although the long periods of celibacy in my life have been as life-giving as they have been lonely. Because of singleness, I have been able to give to many loving relationships instead of one. It is about power. I believe that both singleness and celibacy have potential as revolutionary tools to counter the culture of hetero-patriarchy and capitalism which define acceptable living in terms of proscribed relationships of consumerism (family units). Remaining unpartnered helps me to continue to keep questioning those norms.

So masturbation is not just about pleasure; it is about power – the power to undermine hegemonic ideas about the limits of love. I am grateful to the radicals in LGBTQ movements in the church for opening my mind to these questions. And I am grateful to my feminist mom, who, though she may have had difficulty talking to me about sex, instilled in me the power of being an independent woman with her blue sweatshirt emblazoned, "A Woman Without A Man is Like a Fish Without a Bicycle."

I have been talking about writing this article since I was in seminary. Whenever I mention the title to my women friends, they laugh heartily. Women in ministry want to talk about their sexuality with other women. I am grateful to be one woman for whom this is possible. I often wonder if there are women for whom, when I mention the title of my dreamed-of essay, are like me in the club booth with my girlfriend in D.C. Are they hearing a woman they know personally speak about masturbation for the first time? Are they too shocked and embarrassed to say something about it? If this is you, woman, for God's sake, find a friend and talk about it. What is better than talking about sex with girlfriends? Perhaps you yourself have never masturbated? If you can't bring yourself to talk about it, go buy a book. There are lots of good ones now. Go get a mirror, a cup of warm water and give it a try. Try it; you'll like it. I guarantee it. It may even save your life.

This first piece is one that I am publishing somewhat out of chronological order. I wrote it in 2011. I was in a monastery in a southern Colorado valley desert starting to write my dissertation. I felt pressured to conform my writing to an academic standard that I did not believe would represent my authentic voice. I asked myself, "What is this authentic voice that you feel like you can't express, Julie?" The answer came through an internal voice: "Single and Celibate: How Masturbation Saved My Life." This response was the title of an essay that I had dreamed up in seminary in the mid-1990s, which is why I decided to put this essay first. In a way, it was the seed of my writing voice. At that time, I was part of a crowd of cis-gendered, heterosexual, bisexual and lesbian women who were finding ways of maintaining our sanity in the midst of a patriarchal, misogynist, anti-feminist, heterosexist, homophobic Christian religious institution, The United Methodist Church, in which we all intended to be ordained as clergy. I had an idea that we would all write a chapter for a book about our sexual and gender identity as acts of disclosure and resistance to our church. "Single and Celibate: How Masturbation Saved My Life" was going to be the title of my chapter. I didn't write the essay then and we never published the book. But some 15 years later, in the middle of a southern Colorado valley, when I asked myself what my authentic voice sounded like, the old title came crashing through. I sat down that day and wrote this entire essay, long-hand, on a yellow, lined pad of paper.

Grief Pensée
5.9.2007

Sometimes I am sitting somewhere and for no apparent reason I cry
just some tears not clear
Last time, my spiritual director asks me
    To consider what I am grieving

One morning   I tell myself
    "you avoid this task of grief consideration"
Same morning   someone asks in class
    "Read and write poetry about grief"
    good grief, God is a pain in the ass
    Immediately, I begin to cry   tears from somewhere   don't know why
Only pieces of poetry emerge

Here piecing the pieces:

I have a calculator
It belonged to my best friend, her name is Julie, too

She is a math teacher
the kind of person for whom
Things always add up
She always tries to make calculations when life doesn't add up
Particularly, when life is not fair
The calculator used to be her mother's, her name was Gloria
Julie watched her die in their living room
As Gloria, whose life of personal suffering and caring for others ended
Choked and drowned in the fluid of her cancerous lungs
And in that same living room we planned Gloria's funeral
Where Julie screamed at Julie me because life was not right
and God let the innocent suffer
      She asked if I could tell her why, and I said no.
After me doing Gloria's funeral
in gratitude Julie gave me
A card   An angel to hang in the window   Some marijuana
And the calculator
I use it every month to balance my checkbook
And make sure everything adds up

Here crying, don't know why
Tears add up to something that can't be counted
One long equation
how could it possibly add up?
Grandad and Aunt Edna gone, a generation past PLUS +
Unmet expectations PLUS +
The Church that isn't PLUS +
People who are out – immigrants and queers   PLUS +
War & death, Iraq & Afghanistan PLUS +
Wicked prosper PLUS +
Being alone PLUS +
Sudan PLUS +
Bush? Twice?!? PLUS+
Obama please PLUS+
Iliff eliminates jobs PLUS +
Migrants on the border PLUS +
Addictions that were friends PLUS +
33 young people at VTech PLUS +
Young people without hope I cannot give them PLUS +

Gulf Coast Katrina forgotten PLUS +
Failed perfectionism PLUS +
Ice caps PLUS +
Military state ICE Raids Unwarranted detention Guantanamo
      no habeus corpus PLUS +
      PLUS+PLUS+PLUS+PLUS+PLUS+PLUS+PLUS+PLUS+PLUS+
      PLUS+PLUS+PLUS+
         Nobody seems to care much

When, exactly, am I supposed to stop adding?
      And what does this all amount to anyway?
      Why for most does all this pain add up to nothing?
      Or not enough anyway
      to cause us to subtract just one thing, to sacrifice one iota?
      So that others might add just one thing?
Why am I sitting here crying?
Why isn't everyone crying?
At least tears count for something

Once Vincent asks class
      "Write a letter to loved ones
      Imagine you are about to risk your life for a cause"
I write, "Dear Mom and Dad,"
      my next reaction is to cry
      and I do, though I don't know why
      Maybe because maybe I will die
      Because the Bible tells me so
      "You must lose your life in order to save it"
      Strange math
Next day, Sunday, I am at church
      We sing,   through the flood of warring factions,
                  starving people and despair,
                  who will lift the olive branches,
                  should the threat of dire predictions
                  cause us to withdraw in pain[1]

---

[1] These are lyrics from the hymn *In the Midst of New Dimensions*, written by Julian Rush.

I choke, choke back tears, cannot sing, because, well,
I don't know why,
it feels like the only thing to do

Following Tuesday, I read Brueggemann,[2]
he writes
> That real prophetic criticism begins with the capacity to grieve
> "Because that is the most visceral announcement that things are not
> right... as long as the empire can keep the pretense alive that things
> are all right, there will be no real grieving and no serious
> criticism." (11)

I grieve I cry
> Something/s not right
> Things don't +add+ up
> When I say so
> They tell me
> my math isn't any good
> When in fact
> tears
> +Add+ up to far more
> Than their calculations

"Bringing hurt to public expression is an important first step in the
dismantling criticism that permits a new reality to emerge...
> that cry which is the primal criticism" (12)

> "if the task of prophecy
> is to empower people
> to engage in history
> then it means evoking cries
> that expect answers
> learning to address them
> where they will be taken seriously

---

[2] This refers to a book we were reading for the course Imaginal Education by Walter
Brueggemann, *The Prophetic Imagination* (2nd edition), published by *Fortress Press* in 2001.
Numbers in parentheses are page numbers. Some material in this piece also indicates what I
heard from the book, beyond the literal words I have quoted from various pages.

and ceasing to look to
the numbed and dull empire that
never intended to answer in the first place" (13)

"The empire prefers reasoned voices," (16) not sobs
"…Passion as the capacity and readiness
to care, to suffer, to die, and to feel
is the enemy of imperial reality.
Imperial economics is designed to keep people satiated so that they do not
notice. Its politics is intended to block out the cries of the denied ones. Its
religion is to be an opiate so that no one discerns misery alive in the heart
of God." (35)

I thought that my crying meant something was wrong with me
(and this may very well be the case)
Now I see that my crying also means something is wrong in the world
worth crying about
I will not allow any one or any institution to eradicate my cry/ies

*"The royal consciousness leads people to numbness, especially to numbness about death. It
is the task of prophetic ministry and imagination to bring people to engage their
experiences of suffering and death."* (41)

They have healed the wound of my people lightly, saying, "Peace, peace,"
when there is no peace. (Jeremiah 6:14; 8:11)

"in the center of [my] person and community" I refuse "to fully
embrace the consuming apathy espoused" (40) and the numbness
desired to control me by the institutions that surround

"The task of prophetic imagination[:]
*IS TO CUT THROUGH THE NUMBNESS, TO PENETRATE
THE SELF-DECEPTION…* to *bring to public expression those very fears and
terrors* that have been denied so long and suppressed so deeply that we do
not know they are there." (45)

"I believe
that the proper idiom for the prophet
in cutting through the royal numbness and denial

is *the language of grief,*
the rhetoric that engages the community
in mourning for a funeral
they do not want to admit.
It is indeed their own funeral." (46)

The grief of Jeremiah: for the end of his people, and because no one
would listen and no one would see what was so transparent to him (47)

"… we know from our own pain and loneliness that tears break barriers
… tears are a way of solidarity in pain when no other form of solidarity
remains." (56)

> … such weeping permits newness
> … such weeping permits the kingdom to come
> … such weeping is a radical criticism
> After all, Jesus wept. (57)

"Compassion constitutes a radical form of criticism, for it announces that
the hurt is to be taken seriously." Jesus was compassionate. (88)

> I have compassion on the crowd because they have been with me now
> three days, and have nothing to eat. (Mark 8:2) When he saw the
> crowds, he had compassion for them because they were harassed and
> helpless. (Matthew 9:35-36) When Jesus saw her weeping, and the Jews
> that came with her also weeping, he was deeply moved in spirit and
> troubled… and he wept. (John 11:33-35) And when he drew near and
> saw the city, he wept over it, saying, "Would that even today you knew
> the things that make for peace! But now they are hid from your
> eyes." (Luke 19:41-42)

"In his compassion, he embodies the anguish of those rejected by the
dominant culture, and as embodied anguish, he has the authority to show
the deathly end of the dominant culture. Quite clearly, the one thing the
dominant culture cannot tolerate or co-opt is compassion, the ability to
stand with the victims of the present order. It can manage charity and good
intentions, but it has no way to resist solidarity with pain or grief. So the
structures of competence and competition stand helpless before the one
who groaned the groans of those who are hurting. And in their groans they
announce the end of the dominant social world. The imperial
consciousness lives by its capacity to still the groans and to go on with

business as usual as though no one were hurting and there were no groans."
(91)

> "Newness comes precisely from expressed pain.
> Suffering made audible and visible produces hope,
> articulated grief is the gate of newness,
> the history of Jesus is
> the history of entering into the pain and giving it voice." (91)

Sometimes I am sitting somewhere and for no apparent reason I cry
    just some tears not clear
Crying a long time before something new emerges
    But now the tears – imagination that cannot be co-opted or
    domesticated by hegemonic interpretive power,
    channel of visionary awareness and consciousness (xiv)

> act of radical prophetic criticism PLUS+
> breaking down barriers PLUS+
> voice; suffering made audible PLUS+
> form of art; poetry; metaphor PLUS+
> mourning and lamentation PLUS+
> solidarity in pain PLUS+
> rhetoric that engages community PLUS+
> expression of truth PLUS+
> danger to the empire PLUS+
> compassion for the living PLUS+
> antidote to apathy & numbness PLUS+
> visceral announcement PLUS+
> capacity to care and to feel PLUS+
> enemy of imperial reality PLUS+
> readiness to suffer and to die PLUS+
> funeral for the dead PLUS+

> > Gate of Newness
> > permitting the Kingdom to come
> > thy will be done
> > on earth

Tears +add+ up to a lot

I wrote this piece for a class called Imaginal Education, with Dr. Katherine Turpin. In my long years of education, she was the first professor I had who allowed creative methods of writing and self-expression as valid forms of academic discourse. This piece spilled out of me fully formed with a speed and force that almost alarmed me. This became characteristic of most of my writing in this long, poetic prose style.

Power & Persuasion
April 2008

I have been giving
a lot of thought
lately
To the notion of
Moral Persuasion –
the idea that we have
We, in this case
Being
primarily
Well-meaning
Privileged
White People
the idea that we have
& organize ourselves around
That people can be persuaded

We think
People will be morally persuaded

When
Our cause is righteous enough
Our logic is rational enough
Our argument is strong enough
Our actions consistent enough
Our tone kind enough
Our appeal passionate enough
& so on

We fundamentally believe
People will be morally persuaded
To agree with us
And act in accordance
(these are two different steps
& even if we persuade people to agree,
this does not equal
their willingness to act in accord)

From what I can tell
this "persuasive" strategy
Has rarely persuaded people
at least
not on slavery;
not on women's suffrage;
not on war;
not on nuclear arms;
not on the environment;
not on civil rights;
not, so far, on gay rights;
I mean, in 2004
We could not even morally persuade
General Conference[1]
to state that we disagree

---

[1] This is the global gathering of United Methodists that happens every four years to decide church policies. I have been involved in the movement within the church to change the denomination's anti-queer policies since the year I was ordained, 1996. As of 2019, the only changes that have been made have been for the worse.

When people ultimately decide to change their positions on such matters
It is rarely because they have been morally persuaded
But for other reasons
primarily Economic
Sometimes to save face
"evidence" that convinces
or for other political purposes
especially when to make a compromise
means to avoid meeting more radical demands

Please, persuade me
Give me an example
To persuade me that I am wrong
(& I am not talking about individual instances
where someone changed their mind about something)
when institutions have changed
under the influence of moral persuasion

Moral persuasion.
Why do we keep trying this tactic?
I believe the reason mostly relates to
Our being
mostly Well-Meaning White People

Well-Meaning People believe
that hearts change through moral suasion
Well-Meaning People do not want
to examine the power that holds oppression in place
the material and emotional advantages
that moral suasion does not sway

Examining power means
we are going to have to talk
about what kind of Action,
Not Talk,
Action,
dislodges power
& that's too scary
Too risky

for most Well-Meaning Christians
Challenges our assumptions
about what works
& What doesn't work
Like righteousness,
rationality,
strength,
consistency,
kindness,
passion
The conservative right gets this
What do they do to persuade?
Power, money, threats.
For good reason
We don't want to play that game
But what game are we playing?

One of the reasons
we think these things work
gets at being
primarily
White People (the well-meaning kind)
whose privilege in other arenas
when our whiteness, Christianity, social class
And *not* queerness
gets to define how these things work.
We often do secure the changes or successes we seek
& we think we get these things
Because
We are
righteous,
rational,
strong,
consistent,
kind,
passionate.
When in fact
Our success depends on
The power we have

Because we are
White
Christian
Upper-classed
But we attribute our success to these other attributes
& not to privilege & power

But you say,
"I have seen hearts and minds change."
And, thank God
So have I
But that is not the same thing.
That is individualism
That I can convince you that I am morally right
Has very little to do
with changing the system to reflect that position
White people don't get things
that they want
because they are morally right
White people get what they want because they have
power
& privilege
& do what it takes to protect & keep it

Persuasion &
Power
As a movement[2]
We gotta think about these things some more.

[2] This refers to the progressive caucus organizations within The United Methodist Church working for LGBTQ+ inclusion in the UMC.

My Soul Is Tom Brady
July 2008

Oh, my God. My soul is Tom Brady.
Quarterback of the 3-time Superbowl Champion
New England Patriots
The team for the twenty-first century.
I am New Englandah
Straight from Boston
And I love talkin' smack in Denvah
'bout my teams – Pats, Sox, Celts.
Though Rockies fans can't talk smack about shit.
Weak.

Oh, my God, my soul is Tom Brady.
I used to think football was about
All that is wrong with this world
Patriarchy   Violence   Consumerism
And it is.

I am a feminist and feminists don't do football.
That's what I thought.
But then I realized that I was so fucking serious
About everything in my life
Always *en la lucha*, the struggle
That I took everything so damn
Seriously
(Because this life is no joke, you know)
That I was never having any fun
And I need to relax
And scream my head off
Not just because
I was so fucking angry about this world
(Because this world is no joke, you know)

And then I found football.
And that year we won the Superbowl.
The first of THREE times in one decade.
And I remembered
Growing up
On the couch on Sundays with my dad
Screaming at the television
Watching football.
Defense!!!!! Big D, Big D!
And that was a good memory
That was fun.
And I found myself screaming my head off
And loving Tom Brady
And we won three championships
I swear, just so I couldn't convince myself that I shouldn't watch
And then I realized it doesn't make a ton of sense
To be so dogmatic about shit

I am this.
I am not that.
I am about this.
I am not about that.
I am a feminist.
I don't do football.

Because Tom Brady, he's so
You know, cute.
And I needed to have a heterosexual crush on a jock superstar.
Just to lighten up a bit.
Which I know
Is So, So NOT in line
With radical feminism of any kind.
(And I feel while I am in confession mode that I should also
Confess to Red Sox nation that I have had a sex dream about A-Rod
I know, it's terrible, but it was Really, Really Good Sex.
And while I'm at it, I might as well just admit
So that maybe everyone who is being so judgmental right now can
Fucking Relax.
That when Maria Sharapova, who I do not like,
Because Boston sports fans mostly do not approve of
puss-faced whiners,
(like the Manning brothers)
So when whiny Maria Sharapova
And the Williams sisters, among others, who I DO like,
like, Really SCREAM when hitting that little yellow ball,
Well, it's all quite exciting, don't you think?
Screams that emanate from somewhere deep in women's bodies
Base-level, open-throated grunting by women in public?
Anyway.)

You see, I needed to scream about something
Something undoubtedly
Less important
once in a while.
Just once in a while.
Or once a week,
Or all day Sunday, depending on the game schedule.
You know.
And not be so fucking principled.
I get it Noam Chomsky,
The distracted masses and all.
Manufacturing Consent and all.
Kill Your Television.
The Revolution Will Not Be Televised.

Believe me,
I had that bumper sticker.
And do you know who re-introduced me to football?
A lesbian.
And do you know who I watch football with a lot of the time?
Women.
And some men
Who, though I doubt they would go to the mat
For feminism or feminists
Do solidariously try to be supportive
While deconstructing beer commercials.
My God, they are bad.
The commercials, that is.
Picking beer over women.
Man up.
Some misogyny with that six-pack, anyone?
They do make me think that maybe I should stop
Watching football.

And I heard that when the three-time champion
Superbowl Champion
New England Patriots
Did NOT win
Their fourth Superbowl
Against the less puss-faced Manning brother
That they donated their pre-emptively printed
superbowl champion t-shirts
To Central America.
That also made me think I should stop watching
Football.

And what about the pink gear in support of breast cancer?
The NFL supports breast cancer awareness.
Hot pink shoes
Hot pink gloves
Hot pink sweatbands
Pink ribbons on all-new gear?

Could they give all of that money
for fucking pink consumeristic bullshit sneakers
To some breast cancer research?
Please?
I'd like to think that maybe Tom Brady doesn't do the pink
I guess I've tried not to notice
Because I love Tom Brady
But he probably does.
Because it's that bad.

Anyway.
But my soul is.... Tom Brady.
My soul is.... Beautiful..... paradoxical.... A perfect spiral.... Tough as
nails.... Beloved.... Focused.... Good in the pocket.... A team
player.... Oh, the 2-minute drill, amazing under pressure.... Proud....
Down to earth.... Occasionally injured.... A gamer.... Not a runner....

My soul is....
Ah, my soul IS Tom Brady.

*I began to write this poem at a poetry workshop in which we were asked to
tear pictures that we liked from magazines. From those images we had to
pick one that attracted us the most and put the other ones aside. Then we had
to look at the picture and write a poem, using the picture, starting with the
words, "My soul is.... (the picture)."*

DUMB BITCH
October 2010

"Dumb bitch"
That's what he called me
"You dumb bitch"
Officer McMan
of the Denver Police Department
Right before he put his
cop hands
on my clergy-collared woman's body
That's what he said,
"You dumb bitch."

Before going on I would like to state for the record:
that I AINT NO DUMB BITCH, ASSHOLE.

And him leaning down,
& saying it just that plain

Just for me
in my ear
is what I'll remember the most.
More than the pain that he then went on
to inflict on my white woman's body;
More than him dragging me
on pavement
with his partner
while I tried
to regain my bearings.
More than his response
to my cries
of "Shut the fuck up or I'll break your fucking wrist."
More than his condescending laugh.
More than the appearance
that he seemed to enjoy hurting me.
More than all that,
I'll remember
not seeing his face
for his riot helmet and shield.
But remember
him leaning over me,
as I sat in protest on the ground,
coming close to my face,
my shoulder
my neck
my ear
on my right side
and telling me,
speaking
Only to me,
Man to woman
& saying,
"You dumb bitch"

I felt he picked me
Among other women also picked by police
But me
white

spiritual leader
strong
smart
there
on the street
not in my place
not in a church
but in your face
on your streets
and something in him said,
"No."
He couldn't take it;
could not compute
as man.
So before physical force
The show of brute power
He lowered his voice
Came close to my body
& dominated me first
with his power of language
Backed by a gun.
"You dumb bitch."

I am NOT a Dumb Bitch.

And then he put his hands on me.

DAZED,
They held me
Walked me stumbling
Polaroid shot
Plastic cuffs
Put on a jail bus
With women
Crying
Sitting
They were singing
Holding cell
With women

Talking
Not in touch with my Self
                    or My Body
Some other man cop
took me to be processed
booked
into a room with all the cops waiting.
Processing the arrested.
The cop who led me in shouted:
"Who does this one belong to?"
Who does this one belong to?
WHO DOES THIS ONE BELONG TO?!!!?

I would like to state for the record that I belong to NO MAN.

And then he turned around – McMan.
He saw me.
And he smiled.
And he said,
"There's my girl."
There's my girl?
?!?THERE'S MY GIRL?!?

YOU CALL ME A BITCH
BEAT ME
AND TWO HOURS LATER
I'M YOUR GIRL?!?
FUCK YOU I am NOT your girl.

I got to experience the abuse cycle
On the streets of Denver
With a cop.
#1: You call me a bitch
#2: You beat me
#3: Then I'm your girl
The abuse cycle
Compliments of:
The State.

I should add
That day
WE
In our apparently
Women's and men's bodies
Of many shapes and shades

WE
Were protesting
columbus day
and a parade in denver
that celebrates
among other things
the real history of
the domination of bodies
mostly indigenous bodies
by one cristobal colon
& his minions
millions of bodies
At first the Taino, and then
And then
My pen, it stops here
First the Taino, and then…
I'm afraid I can't complete the list
Don't remember the actual peoples
Despite my education, the ignorance lingers
The actual peoples
The nations I do not know
But I do know the list
IS LONG.
Of bodies
And more bodies

I do not equate my experience
As a 21st century
white woman
Body
With the destruction
Of whole peoples

Mostly brown
Women and men

But there is something
About that voice
That creeping close
To my body
That message

Meant for me
That day
That is a kernel
Of subjugation
of women especially
fundamental misogyny
hatred of women
fundamental building block of this world
the notion
that as man
I will dominate you
by any means necessary

You dumb bitch
You
Are less than me
Under me
Nothing really
But a
Dumb. Bitch. A dog. That reproduces.
And now I tell you so.
And I show you.
So don't forget it,
Bitch.

Not to worry, officer
I haven't forgotten it
Though it may seem preferable to.
No, sir.
I remember

And this remembering
That I am NOT dumb
NOR a vessel created for the reproduction of your species
Believe me, I can be a bitch.
But I am NOT a dumb bitch
OR your girl.

I remember
your voice
your laugh
your weapons
your riot gear
your smirk
your condescension
your lies on the stand
I remember you

I remember. I refuse. I resist.

And though I would NEVER
Thank you
For SHIT.
I am grateful.

For the glimpse
Really just a glimpse
For the knowledge
gained, a glimpse
      In my own body
For the responsibility
      That my body now carries
      That carries with allyship
      Taking risks
      In streets
That this shit is real
That oppression is real
That violence is real
That privilege will not protect you
At all times

That my woman's body
　　Shielded with white
　　Girded with education
　　Covered in Christianity
Still knows
　　I am woman.

So you dislodged my privilege
　　whitechristianclergiedeven
　　And I remembered in my body
　　What it means for woman
　　To be fully woman
　　And be hated for it
And not to take lightly
　　The pain
　　The human pain
That my privilege
Privileges
Normally masks
& that distances me
from the pain
inflicted
on millions and millions
of bodies
on streets
in fields
prisons
behind fences
within factories
skyscrapers
homes
all over the world
pain inflicted
in large part
by my own people
　　white
　　christian
　　u.s.ians

Who wants this privilege
of insulating oneself from pain?
The pain of others?
The pain of humanity?
I guess a lot of people want it
remaining with comfort
made less human
by the disfigurement of distance

The privilege of privilege
The privilege of not knowing
The privilege of not wanting to know
The energy it takes not to know
The energy it takes to shield oneself from such knowledge
& as a result
to never know the experience of the vast majority of the world
to be so disconnected from human reality as to be
completely
and utterly
without
authentic human relationships
What kind of privilege is such denial?

So you dislodged my privilege, motherfucker.
Go ahead and consider it
A Job Well Done.

It did a job on me, it's true
I lived disoriented for quite a while
Realizing
that my privilege would not
protect me
from bodily brutality
especially not
as woman.
Especially if
I seek
Anything More
than surface-level change

Not smiling nicely
asking politely
for some crumbs from your table
But sitting in the street
With others
Of many colors
and a resolute "Fuck you."
Very unlike
A respectable clergy
Woman

But Community and
Spirituality
have restored
my equilibrium
& have restored
your acts of violence
into a source
of resistance
a well of strength
& anger
Full of memories
of community
and crying
& overcoming
To resist again today
And tomorrow.

This reflection describes my experience at a protest of a columbus day parade in Denver in 2007. The American Indian Movement of Colorado has engaged in protest of this parade since the late 1980s in alliance with numerous progressive social change groups. 2007 marked the one-hundredth anniversary of the columbus day holiday, which originated in the state of Colorado. This was published on the blog Post-Colonial Networks, http://postcolonialnetworks.com/ columbuscide-parade-protest-stop-genocide-racism-imperialism-2/. The protest of the columbus day parade in Denver continues. For more information, go to: http://www.transformcolumbusday.org and http://colorado-aim.blogspot.com.

Public Resurrection
November 2010

It's impossible to say for sure
But I think
the first time I ever felt the presence of the Dead
was Hiroshima Day
August 6
Probably 1991, maybe 2
@ the Die-In
@ the A-Bomb Dome.
The only building left standing in Hiroshima to this day
from the annihilation of the first nuclear bomb
dropped on humanity
Lying down next to it
@ the moment of the tolling of the death bell
on the anniversary
8:15 a.m.
A strange feeling came over me
A grieving that was not only my own

While deeply mine
like it was not my own memory
But it was in my own body
A kind of pressing down
This horrible sadness
Presence of people asking why
Asking something
of the live, lying-down bodies

I liken it to the next time
I remember this one more closely
a columbus day parade protest
Denver 2005
Corner of,
right there in front of Coors Field,
Blake and 20th?
The police stopped the traffic
        and the parade
for a street theatre.
And dressed in black
like ghosts,
children, adults floated into the streets
original inhabitants who were killed on these lands
Returned to the streets
        And died again
        Then they killed them right there while we watched
        Crawling and screaming
And then the grandmothers came wailing
over their Dead
        And I could not speak
        But for choking on air and tears
but the Dead were not dead that day either
And I realize
They are Not Dead on any day that someone calls them
With a drum
voices
Or memory
On a street
In a courtroom

They are there
Waiting to be called

on the u.s.-mexico border 2006
        On The Migrant Trail
        We Walk For Life
we also walk in funeral procession in the desert
With white crosses
names of the dead on them
died crossing in that desert
Y también cruces con el nombre DESCONOCIDO
y cambiaba yo ese día con un@ UNKNOWN
that day we were walking in silence
On the black pavement.
In that stretch of road I volunteered to carry strings of
        Tied tobacco pouches, red string tied red cloth
        Pouches, each red pouch one dead adult
That year alone
That one sector of Arizona, hundreds
All red, the Dead
except the white pouches that were tied
were dead children, at least a dozen.
So I carried them, consecrated at the beginning of the camino
and my cross.
I marched behind Steve
Who that day
        Wore a t-shirt
        with the names of the Dead
        from another year
        And I read those names off his back in my silence
walking
And in one moment, just like that, they were all there
I don't know how many
        Just there. Right there.
Grieving and asking, supporting the walking
Of miles and miles and miles
Miles they had walked and not survived
And I was so brokenhearted
        & grateful

But I never spoke of it
because though it was real to me
It didn't seem as if anyone else had noticed

So when in Churchill's court case[1] an elder in the courtroom told me
That every Indian who had ever died from smallpox
Was in the courtroom to bear witness on his behalf
To testify that what Churchill said happened to them was true
To remind us that most people who are alive
do not tell the truth.
Though I was not aware of their presence
I believed this man

Oscar Romero said
That when they killed him
he would live on in the people
& they killed him
& he still lives on
This, I am reminded, is the resurrection
The Public Resurrection
a dangerous resurrection
The resurrection of resistance
Dangerous to forces of power
        to the state
Who would prefer we do not remember
Much less know
Speak to
Be advised by
Our people
The Dead
Who "Threaten Us with Resurrection".[2]

---

[1] The University of Colorado fired ethnic studies professor Ward Churchill, alleging research misconduct. Dr. Churchill filed suit, alleging a violation of his first amendment rights, asserting he was fired in retaliation for controversial speech. He won at trial, but the Colorado Supreme Court overturned the jury's verdict.

[2] Julia Esquivel. "They Have Threatened Us with Resurrection [Nos Han Amenazado con Resurreción]," in *Threatened with Resurrection: Prayers and Poems from an Exiled Guatemalan*. Elgin, IL: Brethren Press, 1982. Pp. 58-65.

Julia Esquivel wrote about the resurrected
Who threaten us with the same
In a poem I read a long time ago
Only now understanding
Peoples whose bodies
Souls
Strength
Spirit
Death
Hope
Suffering
Perseverance
Life
Cannot be taken away from those of us
Who go on living this earthly way
And they teach us
Que ya no hay "que tener miedo a la muerte"
who threaten us to live as the resurrected who do not fear death

I am just now coming to grasp
To understand
Something very basic
For the very first time
That others have known for generations
You would think that I would have known.
About resurrection.
The public kind
Since supposedly this word,
this concept
This movement
Is at the center of my religious tradition
You know – *The* Resurrection
Of Jesus.
But I lost that too
Nothing more than a one-time miracle
For a one-time man
Though others tried to teach me better
I didn't get it
Dead people as a source of life?

source of resistance?
Jesus was precisely this to his people
Is precisely this to his people
no wonder they never taught us this
The living dead are way too much power
for institutions to handle
dead people are not afraid
for obvious reasons
to lose their lives and their things
so they have a lot to teach us about "be not afraid"

Calling on ancestors is not a white protestant tradition
it was not christians who taught me the presence of the dead
Being white, without history, roots, ancestors
robbed me of this knowledge
And I am grateful to have it back
To know
To feel
To experience
What resurrection means
Resurrection of a people
or perhaps
More like
a people who never completely died
(though bodily death is very real)
Unless we let them

It is something that all along I have known without knowing
The power of being in touch with *my* ancestors
My mother's mother
Ann Matilda Brown Krebs Sears
Who prayed for me every day by name
And from whom I inherit
a deep love of the spiritual life
Her husband my grandfather Clarence Krebs
Who baptized me but I never knew
A studious, zealous Methodist pastor
from whom I descended to be the same

My father's mother, Aileen Averill
From whom I like to think I inherited my fashion sense and
an unwillingness, hard fought and hard won
To be abused by any man.
Her first husband, my biological grandfather, George Dougwillo
about whom we never spoke
from whom I inherited not only my alcoholism,
But also, I am firmly convinced,
the gritty
hard-scrabble
working-class anger
that undergirds my relative ease and willingness,
despite my middle-class upbringing,
to tell people to fuck off when it is called for.
And my other grandfather, Bill Todd
the only grandfather I have ever really known
Who would be very disappointed that I swear so much
And is the only person who ever called me by my whole name
Julie Marie
Who taught me that the most important things in life are
hard work   education   and family

I have been thinking lately
How it is important for systems of oppression
That I lose contact with these people
That we lose contact with our people
In very tangible ways
Our history
our communities
ancestors
Those who have been there
& been before
It is important for oppression
for us not to know
this source of knowledge
Resistance
& power

I believe that "the system" does not want to contend with one
  Julie Marie
   spiritually grounded, studious, zealous, evangelical
fashionable-female
   hard-working, well-educated, family-oriented
methodist pastor *and* alcoholic
   Who is unwilling to be abused by any man
   And, in touch with her
   angry, working-class roots
   which empower her to tell you to
go fuck yourself
when it is called for
And that's just one of me,
only two generations removed
from only five of the so-called dead.
No wonder they don't want us to call upon our ancestors, our history.

Nor do they want us to know
Those Horrible things my ancestors
their ancestors
our ancestors have done
Genocide. Slavery. Subjugation. Rape. Exploitation. Should I go on?
Stealing Land. Annihilating Communities. Destroying the Earth.
Should I go on?
Overt and covert wars for natural resources
to support the American way of life?
Should I go on?
Because if we are white, with no ancestors
Then no one can hold us responsible for anything
Because
By God
We're just white
Nobody behind white
This moment seems to call for
My ancestors to empower me to say
No
FUCK THAT.

I want my ancestors.
All of them.
The Resisters and the Horrible Ones.
I want them to threaten to come back to life in me
To live with them
So I have, we have

> Some ground from which to begin restoring this fucking mess
> Strength
> Power
> Wisdom
> Courage
> Honesty
> Source of understanding
> History
> That can remove fear
> The fear of dying
> Because we never die
> Because if we realized that we never die
> Then there are millions of us
> Billions of us?
> With whom
> We can fight.
> Threaten, with a public resurrection.

Confessions of a Christian Supremacist

Originally published in *Reflections: Narratives of Professional Helping*
Winter 2010 (Vol. 16; No. 1): pp. 140–146.

A year ago I enrolled in a social work class called Disrupting Privilege through Anti-Oppressive Practice (for information on the pedagogy and structure of the course, see Walls, Roll, Griffin, & Sprague, 2009; Walls et al., 2009).[1] In the class, students were placed in groups associated with a specific kind of systemic privilege that they personally embodied. There was a white privilege caucus and an able-bodied privilege caucus. Though I shared both of those privileged identities, I was placed in the Christian privilege caucus to

[1] I took this course at the University of Denver School of Social Work with Dr. Eugene Walls, whose teaching and mentoring took me to a new level of comprehending privilege and oppression, particularly the relationship of Christianity to structures of hierarchy. Dr. Walls and I also co-wrote "Defending the Faith: Resistance and Struggle in Recognizing Christian Privilege," in *Conservative Christian Beliefs and Sexual Orientation in Social Work: Privilege, Oppression and the Pursuit of Human Rights*, Adrienne B. Dessel and Rebecca M. Bolen, eds. Alexandria, VA: CSWE Press, 20014: 377–405.

delve into the ways that my Christian identity had benefited me and oppressed others.

Despite my years of anti-oppression work, the language of Christian privilege was completely new to me. I had breathed the air of Christian privilege my whole life. I was a WASP (White, Anglo-Saxon, Protestant) pastor's kid from New England, a former foreign missionary, an ordained local church pastor, and currently a doctoral student in Christian social ethics. I was a serious theological and political progressive, a Christian living on the margins of my own religious tradition. I was a feminist, an activist in my denomination for the full inclusion of GLBTQ (gay, lesbian, bisexual, transgender, and queer) Christians, experienced in interfaith work, and involved in the community for racial and indigenous justice. I was aware of the ravages of Christian domination and violence against marginalized groups throughout the ages. I had no compunction to speak about such matters openly. That it had never crossed my mind, not even once, that my identity as a Christian in this country was a privileged social location was an obvious signal that it was. I did not find it too difficult to accept that the "knapsack" of Christian privileges[2] with which I was associated was, indeed, real: the prevalence and positive portrayal of my Christian tradition and values dominating law, media, culture, and history; the comfort and security of being, speaking, and practicing my Christian faith without threat of violence; and the concrete ways I continue to benefit when atheists and other non-Christian traditions are excluded and marginalized. While I was stunned once again by recognizing this new layer of privilege, my consciousness was raised.

Throughout the first few weeks of the class, I consoled myself with the notion that because of my progressiveness, at the very least, I was "better" than most other Christians. I wanted to clarify that I was *definitely* not like my fellow United Methodists George W. Bush and Dick Cheney. I distanced myself not only from the extremely intolerant, warring-type of Christian, but I was also quick to see myself as different from the other student members of

---

[2] While this list of privileges continues to expand, the first source in which I encountered such a list was Schlosser, 2003.

my Christian privilege caucus, who mostly defined themselves as evangelical.

Certain in-class experiences fostered my transformation. In a theatre of the privileged[3] exercise, I embodied my position of distance from "other Christians." Literally separating myself from my own caucus members during the exercise helped me see that this cognitive behavior was a form of resistance to doing my own work and fully acknowledging the extent of my privilege. While I was distancing from the evangelicals in the caucus, there was some parallel version of this resistant distancing that all of the members of the Christian privilege caucus were actually doing – each of us Christians distancing ourselves from other Christians whom we considered to be somewhere on the spectrum of religiously unenlightened to violently extreme. In fact, my behavior was hardly different. I was also a Christian who considered myself to be a better Christian and better person with better beliefs than others. Disassociating myself prevented me from dealing with a central issue: my own sense of righteousness, how I positioned myself in relation to people of other faiths or no religious faith, and the power wielded by my privileged group over others.

In another experiential exercise, the caucus members participated in a fish-bowl exercise, sitting in the middle of the room while other class members read statements from persons who experienced marginalization and oppression as a result of Christians' attitudes and behaviors. Some members of my caucus cried as we began to bear witness to the anger and pain that our Christian privilege caused among those who were marginalized by our Christian supremacy. I was aware at first that I did not feel more than an intellectual assent to what was being spoken until one person read a statement: "I hate it when Christians think that I would be happier if I only believed what they believe." I felt my body take a defensive position. Somehow I felt accused, but of what? I had to ask myself, did I think people would be happier if they believed what I believed? I didn't want to believe that I believed that. It sounded so arrogant

---

[3] The class instructors used a modified theatre of the oppressed, a pedagogical method first articulated by Augusto Boal using experiential exercises and techniques, to explore the experiences of privilege.

and, yes, privileged. I lived with this question for weeks until I could admit that yes, in fact, I did believe people would be happier if they *at least* believed in God. As I excavated (Kendall, 2006) my beliefs, assumptions, and behaviors, I had to acknowledge that in the past, I had expressed feeling bad for those who didn't believe. Though perhaps more consciously tolerant and less conspicuously imposing, I had to confront the notion that I really accepted as true that my way of believing was superior to others. I had to reckon that I held a deep-down belief that my way was normal, better. I returned to a text we had read early in the quarter by Goodman (2001):

> Superiority is not always conveyed in blatant and intentional ways. In reference to racism, bell hooks… calls this type of superiority "White supremacy." She defines it as, the unconscious, internalized values and attitudes that maintain domination, even when people do not support or display overt discrimination or prejudice . . . . This sense of superiority extends from the characteristics and culture of the dominant group to the individuals themselves. Oppression is commonly defined, in part, as the belief in the inherent superiority of one group over another. (p. 19)

I was coming to terms with the reality that it was not only Bush and Cheney, not only conservative evangelicals, but also *I* that operated in this world with a belief in the inherent superiority of my religion.

It was one thing to recognize that I continued to benefit from the structures of domination that I claimed to oppose. It was another to admit that I maintained those structures with this deep sense of superiority that I would have told you sincerely that I did not possess. Superiority, however well hidden, is still superiority and still imposes its sense of truth and rightness. It is tempting at this early stage of Christian privilege work to paint "the problem" relative to Christian privilege in this country in conservative, evangelical terms. Certainly, the Christian right, in both its theological and political manifestations, is an easy and often necessary target. But seeing only this part of the Christian community as the problem would be to make a similar mistake as locating the problem of racism only in the white South. It does not get at the way in which an inherent religious superiority is deeply and broadly entrenched in most all Christian people in this nation.

A year after this course ended, I was invited to be a facilitator for the next class's Christian caucus. Halfway into the quarter, one of the co-facilitators pointed out that I was able to name easily some of the oppressor positions I embody and maintain – racist, sexist, heterosexist, ableist. Yet she noted that I stumbled when I tried to label the oppressor group with which I had been selected to identify for the purposes of the class. This task of naming had remained unfinished from when I was a student in the class the previous year. In the week that followed, her question stayed with me. In the middle of the week, I heard a radio commentary (Democracy Now!, 2009) reporting on Christian fundamentalism in the officer corps of the U.S. military, particularly as it plays out in the occupations of Afghanistan and Iraq. This exposé described a Christian attitude and practice of religiously motivated domination that was so destructive and horrific that it could be labeled as nothing short of supremacist. I decided to take on the word for myself: Christian supremacist.

The term seemed extreme at first. I had to remind myself that part of my early work on Christian privilege was to not allow myself to distance from the extremes of my own group, a common dynamic in privilege work that Kendall (2006) illustrates in her own struggle where she, as a progressive, anti-racist white person wanted to disown racist white friends and family members. What also made the language difficult to use was how closely it is related to white supremacy. But the previous year's class had shown me how intertwined the project of white supremacy is with Christianity. Part of the tremendous potential of this Christian privilege work is the extent to which it lends itself to work on the intersections of oppression and privilege. While white privilege work connects directly to racial and ethnic oppression, Christian privilege work relates to a whole host of categories of oppression. It not only dominates other religious and atheistic traditions in this country, but is implicated in virtually every other category of oppression: racism, sexism, heterosexism, ableism, classism, and an anthropocentrism that contributes to the destruction of the earth. Every one of these categories has been undergirded by Christian theological justifications. So, it seems even more relevant to call the phenomenon of Christian privilege by this more accurate descriptor named Christian supremacy.

But the intersectionality of Christian privilege work brings up other complications. While Christian traditions and scriptures have served as a source of oppression for many groups, they have also served as a source of resistance and liberation (Cone, 1990; De La Torre, 2002; Goss, 1993; Schussler Fiorenza, 1995). Christianity was the foundation for the system of slavery in the United States and a justification for racism and imperialism for centuries. Yet it has also been a basis for resistance for Africans and African Americans during slavery and the civil rights movement (Morris, 1986). Yet even as the exodus narrative of the Israelites in the Hebrew Bible is a central theme for black liberation theology, it has also been used to justify the conquest and devastation of indigenous communities (Tinker, 2001).

Not only can Christian ideology be mobilized for both oppression and liberation, but there is also within-group stratification that gets played out. White, evangelical Protestantism (both in its historic and current manifestations) has dominated U.S. Christian culture (Marty, 1970; Smith, 1998) and in some cases has served to "other" Roman Catholics in racial terms (Ignatiev, 1995; Miller, 1985).[4] This Protestant supremacy showed itself in the second year in which I participated in the class, wherein both the Protestants and Catholics questioned whether or not the Roman Catholic faith tradition was a Christian tradition. Catholicism has also served as both a source of genocide and oppression for many in this country (Tinker, 1993), and as a source of cultural affirmation and survival for others (Haddad, et. al., 2003). How we sort out these complexities of Christian privilege makes the work especially rich and thorny.

The language of Christian supremacy resonates for me partly because I stand at the intersection of so many privileged identities. Using this language prevents me from distancing myself as a

---

[4] Ignatiev and Miller both document Irish emigrant and immigrant experience in the early U.S. colonies and the United States, including historic evidence of their racialization. Ignatiev documents, in particular, the ways in which the Irish use their European ancestry and whiteness in turn to repress African Americans.

progressive Christian from a tradition of domination whose history and current manifestation is nonetheless mine. I want to affirm the ways in which Christianity can provide special resources for the work of dismantling Christian and other forms of privilege: the prophetic tradition of the Hebrew Bible and the person of Jesus interpreted as confronting oppressive establishments (Campbell & Rosenau, 2009; Borg, 1994). Having participated in two groups of Christians that have started this work, I am encouraged by its potential. Such work is – for some – an aspect of a deeper faith development, an inspiration to learn about other faith traditions, and a call to challenging Christian institutions to greater justice from the inside. Equally as compelling and inspiring to me are conversations coming out of a more radical reading of biblical scriptures encouraged by the challenges offered during the course of the class. For example, such investigations can help begin a process of recognizing the extent to which poverty and economics are at the heart of Jewish and Christian sacred texts (Boff & Pixley, 1989; Hoppe, 2004), and the ways in which Christian individuals and institutions have perpetuated class stratification as much as alleviated it (McCloud, 2007; Rieger, 1998). This can be a foundation for mobilizing Christian ideology, not only for the purpose of disrupting Christian privilege, but for challenging class privilege as well.

Clark (2006) points out, however, that the liberation strain of Christian theology and history makes the identification of Christian privilege difficult in social justice communities. A Christian faith-based *calling from God* to social justice is part of what makes the work of confronting Christian privilege especially hard for individuals. She counsels Christians to recognize the obvious historical limits to the liberative nature of Christian theologies and traditions in their impact on social justice.

There are myriad theological challenges in this work. Obvious among them is the role of the Bible. Many students have not dealt with reconciling traditional interpretations of scriptures that they still hold (for example, the subordinate place of women in family and church or the moral condemnation of non-normative sexual and gender identities) that are in conflict with more just and egalitarian views. The issue of the Bible and its interpretation is most clear as students struggle with what to do with the heart of the Christian tradition itself: the superior claim about the unique saving power of Jesus. The first caucus struggled with the biblical verse attributed to Jesus, "I am the way, the truth, and life. No one comes to the Father except by me."[5] All over the country on Sunday mornings, circles of children are sitting around being taught with this phrase that they are superior to other children who do not come to God by Jesus. Even liberal Christians take such a practice as completely normal and would deny such a verse intends to convey a superior stance. But doesn't it? If we watched a videotape of a white supremacist group training their children that "whiteness is the way, the truth, and the life" we would be completely horrified. So what does it mean for ministers, social work practitioners, educators, and social justice workers to believe in sin, salvation, and hell? At first, some wanted to struggle with how they could continue to embrace these beliefs without seeming oppressive to others. Is there a less offensive but more loving, no less effective way of drawing people into a conversation about faith and salvation? I began to wonder if certain kinds of Christian beliefs and attitudes might be antithetical to anti-oppressive practice. Does a desire to engage in anti-oppressive practice ultimately mean sacrificing such beliefs and attitudes rather than forcing them underground? Many students imagined that rejecting such beliefs was an outright rejection of their faith in God. A dismantling of a privileged identity and its related oppressive institutions seemed a big enough challenge. That this work for Christians may also include dismantling a particular type of relationship with God and disrupting the interpretation of sacred texts seemed another.

The disruption of Christian privilege by challenging certain theologies and beliefs surfaces another unique issue for the work: Christians' training in "defending the faith." The work of disrupting Christian privilege can be taken as an assault on the very framework in which we are taught by certain verses in the Bible that if we are being faithful, we will be attacked. In this line of thinking, "true" Christians are not privileged by the faith, but persecuted for it. This thought was evidenced in students' minds by their experiences of

---

[5] John 14:6

60

what they viewed as hostility and marginalization as a result of their faith expressions during graduate school. The dialogue about these experiences, however, provided opportunity for contextualizing minority religious experiences in the Bible and throughout history that are not comparable to the context of Christian privilege in the United States today. This discussion also served to reinforce another important message that is sometimes difficult for allies (across many axes of difference), that the individual experience of discrimination is not the same as the experience of oppression. For example, while a male student may have a genuine experience of male-bashing from a colleague in a classroom – an experience that is abusive and counter to values of social justice – that does not mean that men as a group are oppressed (for further discussion, see Goodman, 2001).

As I begin to use the phrase Christian supremacist around the halls of my predominantly white, liberal, mainline Christian seminary, most students look at me like I have lost my mind. They primarily deny what I am saying by appealing to the rationalizations I used with myself. I am not the problem. I am marginalized within my own faith tradition. The Christian liberationist tradition is the antidote to oppression. Christianity called me into social justice work. I am not "one of those kind of Christians." Within this institution dominated by the superiority of Christian assumptions, however, those who are not Christian seem to understand exactly to what I am referring. For me, resonance with those who have been marginalized because of religious intolerance and Christian privilege is evidence that there is something true about the Christian supremacy language I am using. If part of the point of doing this work is becoming a better ally in anti-oppression work with marginalized people, then I will take my cues from those who are on the receiving end of Christian supremacy.

REFERENCES

Boff, C. and Pixley, G.V.. (1989). *The Bible, the Church, and the Poor.* Trans. by Paul Burns. Maryknoll, NY: Orbis Books.

Borg, M. (1994). *Meeting Jesus Again for the First Time: The Historical Jesus and the Heart of Contemporary Faith.* New York, NY: HarperCollins.

Campbell, P., & Rosenau, S. (2009, June). "The Pride and Pitfalls of Allyship: On living as a Christian Disciple." Workshop presented at the Pedagogy of Privilege: Teaching, Learning, & Praxis Conference, Denver, CO.

Clark, C. (2006). "Unburning the Cross – Lifting the Veil on Christian Privilege and White Supremacy in the United States and Abroad." In F. Salili and R. Hoosain (eds.) *Religion in Multicultural Education* (pp. 167-214). Greenwich, CT: Information Age Publishing.

Cone, J. H. *A Black Theology of Liberation.* (1990). 2nd ed. Maryknoll, NY: Orbis Books.

De La Torre, M. A. (2002). *Reading the Bible from the Margins.* Maryknoll, NY: Orbis Books.

Democracy Now! (2009). "The Crusade for a Christian Military." Retrieved on 05/11/09 from http://www.democracynow.org/2009/5/6/the_crusade_for_a_christian_military. Based on more detailed analysis of the same issue in the May 2009 issue of *Harper's Magazine* titled "Jesus Killed Mohammed: The Crusade for a Christian Military" by Jeff Sharlet.

Goodman, D. J. (2001). *Promoting Diversity and Social Justice: Educating People from Privileged Groups.* London: Sage Publications.

Goss, R. (1993). *Jesus Acted Up: A Gay and Lesbian Manifesto.* San Francisco: HarperSanFrancisco.

Haddad, Y. Y., Smith, J. I., and Esposito, J.L., eds. (2003). *Religion and Immigration: Christian, Jewish, and Muslim Experiences in the United States.* Walnut Creek, CA: AltaMira Press.

Hoppe, L. J. (2004). *There Shall Be No Poor Among You: Poverty in the Bible.* Nashville: Abingdon Press.

Ignatiev, N. (1995). *How the Irish Became White.* New York: Routledge Press.

Kendall, F. E. (2006). *Understanding White Privilege: Creating Pathways to Authentic Relationships Across Race.* New York, NY: Routledge Press.

Marty, M. A. (1970). *Righteous Empire: The Protestant Experience in America.* New York: The Dial Press.

McCloud, S. (2007). *Divine Hierarchies: Class in American Religion and Religious Studies.* Chapel Hill, NC: University of North Carolina Press.

Miller, K. A. (1985). *Immigrants and Exiles: Ireland and the Irish Exodus to North America.* New York: Oxford University Press.

Morris, A. D. (1986). *Origins of the Civil Rights Movement: Black Communities Organizing for Change.* New York, NY: The Free Press.

Rieger, J. (1998). *Remember the Poor: The Challenge to Theology in the Twenty-First Century.* Harrisburg, PA: Trinity Press International.

Schlosser, L. Z. (2003). "Christian Privilege: Breaking a Sacred Taboo." *Journal of Multicultural Counseling and Development,* Vol. 31, Is.1, 48-49.

Schussler Fiorenza, E. (1995). *Bread Not Stone: The Challenge of Feminist Biblical Interpretation.* 2nd ed. Boston: Beacon Press.

Smith, C. (1998). *American Evangelicalism: Embattled and Thriving.* Chicago: University of Chicago Press.

Tinker, G. E. (1993). *Missionary Conquest: The Gospel and Native American Genocide.* Minneapolis: Fortress Press.

Tinker, G. E. (2004). "American Indian Traditions." In M. de la Torre (ed.) *Handbook of U.S. Theologies of Liberation* (pp. 235). St. Louis, MO: Chalice Press.

Walls, N. E., Griffin, R., Arnold-Renicker, H., Burson, M., Johnston, L., Moorman, N., Nelsen, J., & Schutte, E. C. (2009). "Graduate Social Work Students' Learning Journey about Heterosexual Privilege." *Journal of Social Work Education,* 289-307.

Walls, N. E., Roll, S., Griffin, R. A., & Sprague, L. (2009). Walls, N. E., Roll, S., Griffin, R., & Sprague, L. *A Model for Teaching about Privilege in Graduate Social Work Education.* Manuscript submitted for publication.

Healthy Boundaries
(On containment)
Original Journal Entry 3.1.2011

I HAVE A SPIRITUAL GIFT
a CAPACITY to
CONTAIN EMOTION
some call it co-dependence
and sometimes
That is what IT IS.

Carrying others' emotions for them
HOLDING THEM
     like a container
when they did not ask me to do so
when it is not healthy for
     me to do so.
     but I do it
because that's just how I do

create an emotional dependence
"be there" for people
and less often for myself
I get it.
So I have slowly
       and painfully learned
       from that
       some "healthy boundaries"

I know I need them.

BUT then I Ask
really —
what are "healthy boundaries"
in this world
       FULL OF GRIEF?
with my capacity to CONTAIN EMOTION
what are these
       "HEALTHY BOUNDARIES"?
am I supposed to have
       "healthy boundaries"
in relation to war
       to the pain of war
       the victims of war
       the victims of war perpetrated by my country
am I supposed to put up a boundary
and NOT let that in?

Because that seems to me
       what most of us are doing
       when it comes to
       WAR
       INCARCERATION
       INDEFINITE DETENTION
       TORTURE
       Well, HOW MANY WORDS can I write in one column?

I cannot help but
        suspect that
"HEALTHY BOUNDARIES"
        are white people words
        we of the impermeable denial
a means of distancing
from pain
        and grief
that is all too real
        that requires touch to be healed
        and less so a boundary

It's tricky.

There are two kinds of
        CONTAINMENT
        of which I speak.
TWO KINDS OF CONTAINING EMOTION
        (Maybe more)
        But the two:
One where:
        I hold others and mine together
        like a container
        a vessel
        just holding
        sometimes emptying
        mostly just holding
and another where
        I contain myself
        I contain my own feelings
        I contain my anger
        contain my emotion
        embodying the request
        that inevitably comes
        when someone can't handle
        my needs
        who-how I am, then:
"Hey – put a lid on it."

Put a lid on that container.
The one that I hold for you.
But you don't want any of that emotion inside
backsplashing on you.
Put a lid on it.
and I do, or I did
BUT
not so much
ANYMORE
Enough with lids on my containers.

And here, I've been honored to hold it
But NOW,
you can hold your own.

ANIMAL BODIES
(with all my love to Eli)
April 2011

I lived with a young man named Eli for over four years.
Eli has to be one of the most beautiful human beings
I know.
There is nothing about Eli
that is anything less
than completely real
every single moment of every single day.
Which these days
is refreshing.

Eli has autism.
Severe autism.
He has words
but he does not primarily prefer to use them

He makes sounds

Sounds I cannot describe in words.
Habitual Sounds.
Sounds that
Resonate with his spirit
Express
What IS him
What is IN him.

I live in the basement below his bedroom and his bathroom.
In the morning, I wake.
He wakes.
Morning sounds.
Waking sounds.
Showering sounds.
Pooping sounds.
Not always precisely the same
But in essence the same
Each day I wake, he wakes,
He Sounds
Somehow he expresses
it is morning
and I assent.
The day has begun.
At night,
I unwind.
He unwinds.
Unwinding sounds.
Falling asleep sounds.
Comforting sounds.
Cooing sounds.

There are in between sounds.
Chomping potato chip sounds.
Vacuuming sounds.
Shopping sounds.
Watching video sounds.
Coming home sounds.
Getting ready for a big night out sounds.

Most of Eli's sounds
are happy.
When they are not happy sounds,
they are not happy sounds.
Scary sounds,
Primal screaming sounds
Sometimes with violence
Mostly to himself
Beating Sounds
Head-banging Sounds
Screeching Sounds
and Biting Sounds
Sounds of pain
Sounds of anxiety
        Sounds of Anger
        Sounds of Frustration
That to this human
Say
"I Am Out of Control"
His Mom comments
        Most people do not deal
        Cannot deal well with this
        With this fact
        That in these moments
        Eli
        Is like an animal
        Makes animal sounds
        Is an animal
And no one likes to be reminded
That we humans are
In fact
ANIMALS.

        We have ANIMAL BODIES.
        We are animal bodies
        Animal bodies that we do everything in our power
        To try
        To control
And Eli

And his complete and utter human soundings and emotions
And things like Illness and Death and Nature
      Remind us – not so fast
      Forever we are not actually in control
We ARE Animal Bodies

So we say to ourselves
Must deny this.
Must forget this.
Must use all human faculties
And experimentations
With our bodies and emotions
To make it appear
NOT SO.
NOT SO.
NOT SO.

We are not animals,
We are human.
We do not have animal bodies,
We are humans.
Animals are animals.
We are not animals.
We are not them.
We are not animals.
Animals are not us.
Animals are not human.
Not the same as
US.
Not as valuable as us.
Not in control like US.
We are NOT animals.
Animals are not us.
And if THEY –
Animals –
Are NOT US
NOT related to us
NOT the same as US
NOT as valuable as us

Not alive in the same way that we are

THEN
We can do whatever the fuck we want to them
    Kill them
    Eat them
    Destroy them
        And their habitats
    Cage them
    Exploit them
    Profit off them
    Brutalize them
    Domesticate them
    Objectify them – THEY ARE NOT US.

NOT US.
    We're not animals.
    Humans are not animals.
        Well, some of us are
    There *are* some *human* animals
Criminals, Murderers, rapists, mentally deranged, violent people,
severely disabled

You know,
you know the ones
They're kind of like...
Like...
You know....
Animals?
The human kind that we must
Kill
Cage
Exploit
Profit off of
Brutalize
Objectify
Institutionalize
Domesticate

But not US.
We're not the animals.
Yes we are.
We're the domesticated animals
Whose veil of domestication
Is only broken – lifted
By the connection
To
OUR
ANIMAL BODIES.
When those bodies fail us
When we feel out of control.

Each day I awake
And I arise to the sounds of Eli
The most human being I know
The most human animal I know
And I give thanks to him
That I know
I, too, am an animal.
That if I were only as human as he is
If only I were animal enough
To have access to my most authentic expression and sound
Able with the dawning of each new day
And at its ending
And all the in betweens
to let all my sounds flow free

Ordination Day
(I Shit Myself)
Journal Entry 4.10.2011

On my day of ordination
I shit myself
at breakfast
with the bishop.
We were at UMass
Amherst
in some room.
All the ordinands
deacons and elders
Class of '96
with our sponsors
for ordination.
I was there
with my Dad.
I don't know what
we had for breakfast

or even if we had
eaten yet
or not.
And I felt this rumbling
in my gut,
you know,
like
serious intestinal
Movement.
And I thought I
could hold it
but I could not.
If I had waited
2 seconds
longer
I would have had
One Serious Mess
right there
at the bishop's breakfast.
But I made it
to the bathroom
though barely.
By the time
I hit the stall
it was on its way
out
Yellowy-brown
Shitty
Runny
Diarrhea
All in my underwear
and my stockings
and all on my bum
my legs.
I was like
Oh my god
oh my god
And I just cleaned
myself

and obviously
pooped it all out
and I was missing
the bishop's breakfast
and I thought
"I gotta get back there."
So I cleaned
and threw away
my underwear
& nylons
in the trash
and went back.
And my dad
looked at me, like
"What happened?"
And I was like,
"I had to go –
        bad."
And I chalked
that shit
up to
Nervousness.
And I never
spoke about it
to anyone.
Maybe by this
point
I've told
two people.
I don't even know
Who.
People I guess I thought
should know.
Because otherwise
it was something
I was completely
Ashamed of.
I shit myself
on my ordination day.

Occasionally I
have thought about this,
what it meant,
Really.
Perhaps I have even
written about it
in the past.
I can't remember.
But it returns to me today.
a day I am thinking
again about ordination
something
I have thought a lot about
recently
like
well
since I've been ordained
but especially in the
last five years.
At one point
I thought
it was Over.
God put me through
a horrible wringer
of surrender
& I went through
grieving and letting go
and telling my family
and close friends
and Then
I felt
that God
for Some Reason/s
after all that
was not really
asking me
to give them up,
my orders,
that is,

after all.
And the only thing
I have made
of why
I had to go through
all of That
was so that I
would be in
Right Relationship
with those things,
that thing,
Called
"my orders."
And so God
Did
"that thing"
For that reason.
But when I return
to ordination
and the thought of it,
the Why of it
The
        "why am I still ordained?"
of it.
For some reason
I return to
Shitting Myself.
Which somehow seems
incredibly fucked up
but nonetheless
important.
And the thing I keep
returning to
is that somehow
ordination
is a calling
that is worth
shitting ourselves for.
like if those of us

being ordained
knew what calling
really entails
We would all
      Shit ourselves.
From fright.
Of what God
might possibly
Demand.
And I wonder
If somehow
Deep Down
I knew that.
Consciously –
I did not know what I was getting myself into.
Being a pastor
and all that.
Really,
even with all I knew.
I didn't know.
how hard
it would be
But its really
      More than that.
What Deep Down
I knew.
It's probably that
what I knew was that
Deep Down
What god was calling me to
wasn't quite this
whatever "this" – being a pastor
Was.
But I knew
that in this calling
that was very real
& still is
that being a pastor
could not contain

the calling
I deeply had/ve.
That being a pastor
would not allow me
to truly express
to creatively express
the depth of that calling
the part that will make you shit your pants.
Somewhere I knew
that answering the call
in this way
would only be answering it
in part
and parts would be
Cut Off.
I would not answer
all of the call.
I would contain
It.
I think I knew
in some way
that in those moments
even of answering
an honest call
I was also
shutting down
parts of myself.
I knew it
And it made me sick
And my body said
"no."
And I shat myself.
And I called it nervousness
and I returned
To the bishop's breakfast.
I think I left the local church
for, well, among many possible reasons
because I could no longer
shut down parts of myself

no longer contain
the calling
that continues to desire
to express itself
but what my calling
as far as ordination goes
is
I do not know
I feel as if
God has me have these things
these orders
for a reason
that I
do not know.
And that's okay.
But I do wonder about it sometimes.
I do know
that I am
a spiritual leader
a spiritual leader
of some sort.
I do recognize
That I have
Gifts and Graces
as a pastor
a priest.
I do know
that God called me
through the eucharist.
I do know
that God moves in me
through ritual.
I do know
that I loved my people,
and,
for the most part,
they loved me.
I do know
that the church formed me

and has given me a space
and language
and authority
to speak
as pastor
as prophet
And I am grateful
to the church
for making me
who I am.
But I feel
that you
cannot contain me
any longer.
And I don't know what this means.
Still,
at this moment
I do not feel moved
to give up my orders.
But if there were a reason
I feel
I would.
I have been
through that process.
And perhaps it is just me
& my fear
that I just don't do it.
That shitting myself in the first place
Was just a 'no'
that I should have responded to
Then.
Or maybe I am just waiting
for the shit to hit the fan.
That when I finally came
come to the place
of responding to
the deeper calling
that causes me
to shit my pants

literally
or figuratively
my calling
my ordination
will become clear
and I will live into it fully
or I will let it go.
Or perhaps
those two things
will be the same thing.
Once again,
        I don't know.
I feel
I know
the calling
is related
        in a way
        to being
        of being
        prophetic
        a prophet.
That was certainly a piece
within the pastoral work
that I always
felt I contained
        even when church people
saw my activity in community
heard my voice prophetically
and resisted me in that role
whether over war
or gay stuff
or racism
or whatever.
As much as I raised that voice;
As far as I was active in community;
As far as I embraced that role,
I rarely said
as much as I wanted to say
I rarely told

the whole truth
I often stopped short
and spared people,
spared myself
I guess.
You want a prophet?
read Isaiah.
Really Read Isaiah.
Isaiah will make you
Shit Your Pants
and this is the calling
perhaps
of which I am afraid
that kind of speaking
that will cause you
to shit your pants.
because the world is just that fucked up.
And most everyone knows it.
And the church?
Knows it.
Caused it.
Profits off it.
In every way.
And therefore
God
doesn't give a shit
for what we do
anymore.
and we
will be
destroyed.
And that's it.
And so who
would like
to share
that message?
Please, please,
Pick Me.
But let me first

go shit my pants.
Fortunately, there is another side
to Isaiah.
and if
indeed
that kind of prophesying
is my calling
I will be as poetic
about the comfort
and the joy
as the destruction.

The Deer
12.20.2011

If it had been a split second later, I might have missed it. I was in a hermitage in a desert valley in Crestone, Colorado, on a cold December morning. I was sitting on the toilet. Auspicious. Out of the corner of my eye, I saw a sudden commotion – a fast-moving animal outside. I jumped up and looked out the window. Perhaps 150 feet away, I saw the coyote. Gray. Long tail. In an instant, it jumped up and latched onto a deer's neck. Although it was a small deer, it was probably three times the size of the coyote. Another three or four deer charged the coyote and scared it off. It trotted a few feet away, but then quickly turned and charged the little deer again, who stood there sideways, maimed and shocked. It didn't even fight when coyote got its neck again. It stumbled. The coyote held on, rascally and vicious. It hung from that deer's neck, jaw locked. The deer walked-stumbled. The coyote held on. The other deer ran around and charged it again. The coyote held on, and the deer fell. It held on until the little deer was good and dead on the ground. Strangled it. A few other deer family drew near, I think, to make sure that deer was dead. It was. Dead.

More deer showed up, milled around at a distance, and eventually gathered on a rise above the spot of the killing. As if they had called one another. Eventually, some thirty deer gathered up on the rise. Stood there. Ears up. Occasionally one or two ventured down to check on the dead deer, make sure again their friend was dead. They must have stood their deer vigil, dozens of them, silently, for at least four hours.

I was glad I couldn't see precisely how it went down after that. The main part of the deer carcass fell behind some brush. I couldn't see the deer, except for the head and a general sense of its body. But from that point on, the main action was watching the coyote tug, tug, tugging, yanking on that deer. Ripping it to shreds. Then the birds started showing up. Pretty quickly, all at once. Magpies. Scavengers. The birds surprised me. My romantic notion of these beautiful creatures was dashed. In between tugging, the coyote scared off the magpies. Then big, black birds – crows or ravens, I'm not sure which. All of the birds tried to land on the deer to get their piece. Probably for a half an hour – coyote tugged, pulled, yanked, chewed, ate, and ran off the birds. Birds circled, waited in trees, and occasionally attempted another swipe at a piece of meat. One coyote. Tugging, pulling, chewing. Dozens and dozens of birds.

I was surprised more coyotes didn't show up. Besides the birds, the coyote ate alone for quite a while. Eventually, it went up on the opposite rise from the deer vigil. The only thing I noticed about it was its wet, skinny legs, dark from the blood. It seemed to look off in the distance. I didn't see or hear it howl or bark. Another coyote arrived. The first stood off while the second one ate. I only ever saw two coyotes at any one time. As time went by, that deer ended up in four different places: body, head, limbs. I felt slightly queasy once when I saw one of the two coyotes was dragging the head. The birds got to have their way with the rest of the pieces and parts.

After a couple of hours, I forced myself to the task of reading and writing – the reason I was in the hermitage in the first place. Occasionally something would catch my attention, and I would stare again for a time. The deer were still holding vigil on the rise.

Back to writing. At one moment, I became aware of a massive black-brown wingspan rising up from the carcass, and I watched the coyote back away. The awesome bird raised its wings once, twice, three times, then seemed to settle down. I had no idea what it was. Someone said it may have been a turkey vulture. Another said the turkey vultures had gone, so it must have been a golden eagle. I had not seen it land, and I did not see it go. But the wingspan. I will never forget the majestic wingspan.

It was almost sunset when I looked up and realized I couldn't see the parts of the deer lying around anywhere. There was no action at all. No birds. I couldn't see anything. I decided to go outside and take a look. I was nervous about seeing the leftovers. That might be the worst. But with every step closer, I realized there wasn't anything there. It just looked dirty. It didn't even look like blood. It was more like dirty snow. There was nothing. No skin, no bones, no entrails, no hooves, no ears, nothing. Nothing. There was nothing in that snow. I could not believe it. The animal world took the whole deer away. Clean. Gone. As if nothing happened. I did not feel a special energy. It did not feel sacred. It did not feel like death. It was as if it did not happen, but for the dirty, brown snow.

I heard no sounds associated with the whole series of events, except for the occasional cawing of birds. It was completely intense and full in its quietness. That's the thing. It was wordless. Entirely without words.

I knew I wanted to write about it, but it took me several days to start. I had thought about writing for a few days. But I couldn't. I wondered why. Then I realized why: I didn't have words because there were no words. One night, after watching the waning, glowing pink sunset, eating dinner, that's what I thought: I can't write about it because I don't have the words.

I had watched a coyote kill a deer. I might have been horrified. Except for the people who lived at Nada Hermitage, everyone else I had spoken to about the event thought it was disgusting. But here's what I didn't know how to describe. It was awe-inspiring. I knew I was watching something real and violent, yet I felt dispassionate about it. Like it was not the most horrible thing I had ever seen, though in a way it may have been. The pulling, the tugging.

Different parts of the deer in different places. The birds flying off with pieces of meat in their beaks. It was grotesque. But I was surprised that my own human sensibilities were not more offended. It was something I was a simple witness to, honored to see.

At the time of this event, out of the window at the very desk where I watched this all take place, I was literally in the middle of writing a doctoral dissertation on violence and (non)violence. I was engrossed in words, words, and more words. I was working on a chapter discussing the tensions in the moral quality of violence and (non)violence for social change and the matter of if and when violence is justified in the cause of fighting oppression. I realized that I had just watched an act of violence that was completely lacking in moral quality. There was no morality or immorality in this act of nature. It simply was. In fact, the violence was part of the necessity of creation. There must be violence for there to be life, for beings to survive. I had read this very thing in *A Language Older Than Words* by Derrick Jensen, who was one of the interviewees for my dissertation. When frustrated by coyotes and his dogs killing his chickens, Jensen wrote about what he learned from the cycle of life and violence, about interspecies communication and the honoring of the wisdom of the animals. If you need to kill in order to survive, in order for you and your relatives to survive, then you may need to kill in order to survive. It is not necessarily a matter of morality. Or maybe it is for humans. But the natural world shows us that in order for some beings to live, others must die. It just happens that way.

Acts of human violence are so fraught with provocation, words and reactions, extreme feelings, and more reactions. Our reactions to the reactions. This act of violence in the desert simply was. It was not some emotion-laden over-reaction or analysis. In terms of my human projection, the only thing that made me emotional was watching the vigil of those thirty or so deer, standing up on the rise, at attention, for hours. The little deer was gone in an instant. Yet there they stood, watching. No words. Even as I sit here and try to put words to what I saw, what I experienced, I don't really have the words. None of these words will do. At all.

I went out to the site again the night I began to write, at sunset when there was still enough light. I stood there, awkwardly, wondering if there were words. There was fur. Quite a bit of it here and there. I hadn't seen it before. Perhaps the first time I thought I would see blood and gore and when I didn't see that, I didn't see anything. The other thing I saw was urine. That's what I was doing when I first saw that coyote through the bedroom window. Urinating. I wondered if the coyote urinated all over everywhere to mark the territory, the kill. Or have all the other deer been urinating all over everywhere in sanctification and protest?

I saw something unique and amazing for a human to see. I was connected to that deer and coyote, as a witness. It was a kill in the creation, and I saw it. No moral judgment. Just being there. I didn't have a great feeling for coyotes afterward, but I realized they were just doing their coyote thing. Again, no judgment.

There seemed to be some meaning in it all. At the same time, I don't want to impute some human meaning to where there is simply the reality of creation. I used to need to understand scriptures like "The mountains are declaring the glory of God" literally. Now I think, "Well, maybe." The mountains may be declaring the glory of God. I'm all for that. But maybe the mountains are just being mountains today. Full of mountain-ness. Declaring? Perhaps. I'd love to hear what the mountains declare, and if it's the glory of God, that would be great. But if not, I'd like to hear what else. I used to have to objectify every single thing in nature with my human, sacred interpretation of it. Now I try just to let life and death be.

There is a similar dynamic with my thinking about the deer and the coyote. In my humanness, I am prone to think and emote, "Oh, I wish the coyote hadn't killed the deer. What a horrible thing I saw today." A certain interpretation of the scriptures tells me that in God's glorious future, "The coyote will lie down with the deer" like the lion lies down with the lamb. But why do I need for this to be true? That day I saw a coyote kill a deer. It offended my human sensibilities just a little bit, and I think that is probably a good thing. I felt that I was a witness to the way things really are. It was not an affront to the way things should be in God's present or future world. I experienced a creaturely connectedness, which need not add overly imputed meaning with human words. I feel honored to have witnessed this event and to have gained this important knowledge from it. To make meaning, but not too much. To not put too much into words, though now I have.

Spirituality and Service

Published as "A Ridiculous Frivolity" in
Desert Call: Contemplative Spirituality and Vital Culture
Volume 12, No. 1, Spring Edition 2012

As I sit and ponder the notion of spirituality and service, I am in the middle of a southern Colorado desert, mostly alone, for weeks. I stare at a decreasingly golden, increasingly dark blue evening sky that frames the distant San Juan Mountains. I sit curled on a bench in my hermitage, gazing at a waxing crescent moon and its immaculate relationship to the sparkling Venus on the western horizon.

I think of my life in Denver as an activist and student, a teacher of religion and social change. Always a cause. Always an issue. Always in the struggle. Always serving an organization on the margins of survival, whose people are on the margins of survival. I am a radical. I strive to live a life of radical service.

So what ridiculous frivolity is this? Sitting out here in the middle of the desert staring at the night sky? When there is work to be done? While people are suffering? What am I doing out here?

I sit here seven years past serving ten years in pastoral ministry. I left local church work after burning myself down to the ground time and again. I have always identified a call to prophetic ministry. As a pastor I was also a community activist. I lived my life committed to serving others in my church and community every day. The work never ended. I tended to the words of the founder of my denomination, John Wesley, who said: "Fix some part of every day for private exercises. You may acquire the taste for what you have not: What is tedious at first will afterwards be pleasant. Whether you like it or not, read and pray daily. It is for your life. There is no other way, else you will be a trifler all your days, and a petty, superficial preacher. Do justice to your own soul; give it time and means to grow. Do not starve yourself any longer."[1]

I was no trifler. Not in work and not in prayer. I practiced daily prayerful exercises. I would have told you I felt close to God, and I believe that I was. At the very least I am sure that God was close to me. A practice of daily prayer allowed for that possibility. But I was starved. I was over-committed and exhausted. The prayer life to which I was committed was not enough to balance the life of service I led. I did not do justice to my own soul. I hadn't really listened to it in years. I sought out periods of extended quiet like a drowning woman coming up for gasps of air; floundering, close to going under, but alive. I had very little sense of my self, except that I was very, very tired. Short periods of time away allowed for the minimum of required bodily rest. It was better than nothing. I hardly knew any pastors who took significant time off. What would our communities do without us? By God, I was serving the people.

The first time I took a week-long silent retreat, God took the one chance I really gave God to intervene. In the most loving way imaginable, God cracked me into a hundred pieces. I couldn't do it any longer. My life of service was no longer sustainable. Since then, God has showed me how to piece my prophetic call and life of service back together again.

---

[1] Letter from John Wesley to John Trembath, August 17, 1760.

It *is* a ridiculous frivolity to be sitting out here in the desert. I recognize that it is a privilege born of much privilege. But it is a frivolity that my soul requires, that I cannot *not* afford. I want to be an activist. It is in my blood. I want to live my life as a radical, in radical service to others. I believe it is the most meaningful form of living, and the one that Jesus requires of me. And if I want to be a radical, then the most radical, counter-cultural act is to come out here in the middle of nowhere and tend to my own soul. For a long time, radical only meant to me to be out in the world and intensely active to counter the evil and oppression of systems. The intention of these systems is to stifle and destroy the humanity and divinity of individuals and community. Resistance to these systems takes work and sacrifice.

The word radical relates to the word root, something at the base, which is fundamental and essential to the character of something. I buy into the system that destroys life when I allow it to rob me of my own fundamental, essential humanness and divinity. I allow this when, in my incessant activity to change the world and confront destructive systems, I make no room for the fundamentals of being human and resting in God. I virtually reflect the economic and political systems I claim to oppose by replicating its life-and-spirit-denying character: work-produce-accomplish, work-produce-accomplish. A radically spiritual time and space actually cultivates that which hopefully becomes truly socially radical – the spirit of creativity, resistance, confrontation, innovation, subversion, transformation.

The suffering of this world, both human and non-human, is critical at this stage of our history. If one does not tend to the soul with the utmost expansive of practices and time, one will starve to emotional, spiritual, and physical death. This may sound like hyperbole, but someone who is reading this knows what I mean. Survival and thrival in these times also requires investment in cultivating and building community with others so radically committed, both spiritually and socially. Solitude and contemplation, in daily life and on retreat, impacts family and friendship relationships, community, work, and income. These are all questions of the spiritual life. We must build communities that will sustain alternative family and support systems making these periods and practices possible. Affirming radical, bold community, where individual and collective work go hand-in-hand, is also radically political and counter-cultural. I will not be that person who starves myself spiritually, all alone, while venturing to serve. A daily practice is critical – as John Wesley pointed out – for life. But I have discovered that it is not actually enough for a life of radical, sacrificial service. With the same amount of seriousness of devotion, emotion and time I take to serve, I have to tend my soul.

I have needed regular retreat for so many reasons. When I listen more to God, I listen better to humans and non-humans. I am more present. The expansiveness of the natural world where I have been attracted to retreat has expanded my interior space. I have a greater capacity for feeling my own pain, my own sadness, my own joy. Therefore, I have the growing capacity for spaciousness with others – the spaciousness in which to laugh, the spaciousness in which to sit, the spaciousness in which to share suffering. I have the ability to wait. I need this sky, this moon, these mountains, this planet. These mountains have taught me to think long-term. The moon and stars and land keep my human perspective and my own sense of importance in check.

God takes these longer periods of time in the magnificence of this creation to check in about exactly who I think God is. A life of service is so fraught with the seduction of a savior complex, it's not even funny. In the past I have been dying on the inside while attempting to save the world on the outside. Slowly, I am dying to the ego-serving self of service. So many of us Christians are tempted to an overly grand servant role, especially those of us who are professionals. When I serve my spiritual self, I put myself more clearly in the service of God and more genuinely in the service of others. In periods away, I realized that many of my motivations to serve were addictions to my unhealthy need to be liked, respected, affirmed, and valued for my actions: work-produce-accomplish, work-produce-accomplish. I often felt resentful of and superior to those who were not working as hard as I did. I would have denied it then, but I occasionally enjoyed being a martyr for the cause, the suffering servant. No one worked as hard as I did. No one cared for others as much as I did. No one was as committed as I was. Though they still rear their ugly heads now and again, I am glad to turn my back on those unwanted behaviors who were close companions.

Now I genuinely ask for God to guide me into avenues of serving and doing justice that are truly callings and not seeking for approval or recognition. My service is less and less about me, my need to be needed, my excellence as a caregiver, or how down I am with the struggle. It is important to realize that I am not critical to the survival of "the movement," my church, or the universe. Truly, this is a relief. While I seek the spirit, the world continues to turn without me, and I am more present to serve when I return. These spaces and times have taught me to know and to laugh at my own sense of self-importance. I have learned, thank God, to lighten up. I have even learned that a serious, hard-working, non-trifling life of service might include, of all things, serious trifling.

It used to feel to me like the life of service and the spiritual life were discontinuous. Going on retreat was being "away" from "life." Retreat recharged me for living and for service. This is still true in many ways. Yet strangely and hope-fully to me, longer periods of quiet and solitude have begun to feel less discontinuous with the "rest of life." It has enlivened my daily prayer. Daily prayer has become more a place of sustenance. My regular private exercises become more thoroughly infused with the expansiveness and spaciousness of longer periods of solitude. They provide me with more access to the time and means to grow. I no longer spiritually starve. The life of service and the life of spirit are starting to come together for me in unimagined ways. This feels deeply radical. It has led me to a place of anticipation in my life in which I cannot even imagine the paths of radical spirit and service on which God may ask me to walk.

THIS CREASE IN MY BROW

Published in *Rain and Thunder: A Radical Feminist Journal of Discussion and Activism* (Fall/Winter 2012): pp. 22-23.

This crease in my brow
right in between my eyebrows
a little bit closer to the right brow
than the left
One might call it a wrinkle
in my aging face.
But it's more than that.
It's a crease,
deeper than a wrinkle
It bothered me when I first noticed it.
I was
looking in the rear view mirror in my car one day.
"It means I'm getting old"
was one train of thought
That engrained cultural horror of
Women in this country

Like wrinkles are a sign
That one has been deficient
Generally, for showing signs of age
Or in facial care specifically
No longer beautiful
If she ever was
I can talk myself out of all that bullshit
Though it takes a while

No, this crease,
it struck me, was definitely
a result
of seriousness.
A kind of frowning concentration,
an intensity of thinking,
of reading
of not understanding
and understanding
    the way/s the world is
    culture of violence
    particularly for women
    patriarchy ain't no joke

On the one hand it also indicated ·
Something I have known for a while now:
That I have been a bit overly serious
in my life
and need to lighten the fuck up
So when I notice my crease
I think
"Lighten the fuck up, Julie"
But on the other hand
It reminds me
That
Life is serious.
There is serious shit going on on the planet
      & for women bodies of all kinds and ages
that requires serious thinking
and serious action

and I am seriously serious about
being one of those people
who takes life
and the world
seriously.
With determination.
Consideration.
Deliberation.
Resistance.

Then one day at the gym though
Drying my hair
Looking in the mirror
I noticed a set of wrinkles
Like 2 or 3 particular lines
under my left eye
more towards my temple
And I thought at first
"MORE!"
Aging.
And then it seemed like these wrinkles were
in a strange place.
Like, how did my face so regularly move
So as to create these indentations?
And then I smiled
And there it was
There was actually a whole
HUGE
set of wrinkles
on that side of my face
to the left side of my left eye
And those few I first noticed
Were just the ones
That remained
When I relaxed my
facial muscles.
After smiling.
And I thought,
"Good."

Signs of JOY
Smiling and laughing
In community
        with womyn
        all of us aging
& resisting
Amidst the seriousness
of struggle

It does
Leave
some marks

Offering My Heart to God
Journal Entry 12.3.13

I realize I need to make
An offering of my heart
To God
Which only seems somewhat
Obvious
When I say it
Like, I'll take it out of my chest cavity
Every day
And hold it out and up
To God and say,
"Here it is,
I need some help with this today,
Okay?"

I am oatstraw
Journal Entry 3.21.13

I am good alone
I am strong
I am vital
I am steady
I stand tall
I provide
>   Fruits
>   Wisdom
>   Sustenance
>   Steadiness
>   Strength
To others
On my own,
I am
Life giving green
Milky goodness
Food for body and mind.

I am flexible
I am nourishing
I am present to others
I am good
      Very good,
      Alone.
But my added strength
Perhaps my best strength
    My best quality
Is what I bring to others
Being fully me
While balancing out
Blending
Adding the same
Strength and
Steadiness
Juiciness and vitality
That are my hallmarks
To my other
      Relative herbs
      Friends and lovers
In their extreme qualities
Where they need softening, mellowing
Support
Nurture
Moisture
      For their harder
      Acidic
      Astringent
      Bitter
      Ways
At the same time
      I love to be blended
      With them
      To take on
      And take in
      Absorb
What they have to offer me
      Their taste

Their qualities
Their flavors
Their quirks
I enjoy being enlivened
By them, through them

As I take them in,
They build on my strength
My steadiness is their
        Building block

I am oatstraw
        I can and do stand alone
        I am good alone
        But perhaps better with others
        Indeed, I crave to know others
        And to be known

I am *avena*
        You do know me as Oats
        Hearty
        Textured
        Comforting
        And filling
I am *avena sativa*
I am cultivated
        Come with me
        Let me cultivate
        The fullness that is you
        With the fullness that is me
Take me in
Taste me
        My slight, milky sweetness

I will be good to you
Powerful, subtle
Sensitive, wise
You will not be able to deny me
I will transform you

You may not know it yet
But you need me
And I need you
To bring out my juicy, flowing self
Let me lighten you
Let me loosen you up
Let me massage you
And the deepest desires of
  Of your flesh
  And your spirit
Come unto me
Move with me
Move into me
One with you
I am oatstraw.

While living in Denver, I had a stomachache and no health insurance. I received herbal treatment for the first time. I was so intrigued with this healing experience that I took my first course on herbalism. Cultivating a relationship to plants and their medicine set the stage for significant shifts in my physical and spiritual health. In the first long-term class on plant medicine that I took with my teacher Tonja, we did a guided meditation in which we visualized meeting a plant that would become our ally throughout the course. I met oatstraw, whom I had never heard of before. Over the course of eight months, I got to know oatstraw intimately. I wrote them lots of poems. This was one. Whenever I wrote about oatstraw, s/he was also writing about me.

Cultivating (*Sativa*) Desire
Written in honor of Oatstraw (*avena sativa*)
Journal Entry 3.24.13

Sometimes I wish
that my desire/s
would just explode
upon my consciousness
and life
like a juicy bomb
of love & excitement
That God would descend
more like a squawking
gliding hawk
instead of descending like
a gentle dove,
and drop a revelation bomb
on me
about my future.
That what I should do

with my life,
that the desires of my heart
would become crystal clear
in the wreckage of my
revelatory explosion.
Or that the man of my
dreaming & desiring
would finally just show up
one day
and declare,
"It's me,
the one you have been waiting for,"
And there would not be a doubt
love at first sight
desire so obvious
handed to me like a gift.

That all would be super great.

And I actually know it is possible
because God
has sent
such gifts of clarity
to me
on a few occasions.
Though it is easy to romanticize
now
how welcome those gift/s were(n't)
at the time.

And I suspect
these days
as a new period in my life
unfolds,
that the process of uncovering desire/s
feeling them
determining them
embodying them
may be more subtle

more slow.
Because I actually
have many, many desires
and dreams
that are worth
living with, over time.
And perhaps God
(well, surely)
is working with me to
cultivate (thank you, *avena sativa*)
cultivate desire.
Cultivation takes time
takes care
intention.
One does not cultivate
with a bomb.
The cultivation
of the spirit
by the spirit
of deeply held desires
and dreams
might be expected
to take work,
internal & external
work.
Less like a flat-out gift,
freely given,
and more like
opening a series of
wrapped and buried
gifts
that when discovered
and freed
allow for life
to be lived
freely and with joy.
It would be nice
if my desires and dreams
might be handed to me

on a silver platter.
And in many ways,
my life has been so filled
with goodness
that
it feels in the moment
like it has been so.
But actually
if life itself
were not struggle
and testing,
experiments
and striving,
seeking and finding;
if life's dreams & desires were handed to us
on a silver platter,
or dropped like a bomb,
either way,
there's a good chance
that we would not appreciate it.
That we would appreciate
life
less.
So let me cultivate my dreams
my desires
let them rise up in me
over time, and
with intention and
awareness
for the wonder
that is life
and all it gives
when we are open to it
and reverent
in the awe
of its slow unfolding.

A Letter from and to My Body
Journal Entry 2.10.14

From my body: Dear Julie, You are a goddess. If only you knew that deeply from within. Thing is, you do know, and you are just trying to get there. You have been occasionally pretty hard on me, your body, but no more so than you have been on the rest of your so-called self. And yes, it is time to really stop some of that hard-core pushing; to lighten up, to soften, and let your true self really shine without all of these outside forces determining for you who you should be, how you should look. I do know better than anyone the extent to which your working out has been obsession – pushing yourself, pushing me to some unnatural, for me, limits. My type of body is not really prone to being hard. But actually it is good that through this obsession you really have learned about your health, your boundaries, who you are – which is beautiful. You have been hard on me. Please be more kind. I need more rest than before. That's just the reality of it. I am speaking a bit of my anger through your back, and yes, sadness too. You are listening now. Give yourself credit for that. You have always had this deep capacity to stop and listen to me, a capacity most people are not even aware of, much less do they practice. All I want is for you to listen. And yes, there are deeper messages for you that dwell in me than just rest and listen. But you are not going to access those deeper messages without first dealing with some of the literal and figurative pain I hold. Yes – those damn layers. But I know you know – doing this work is about freedom, your joy. Yes, I want someone to touch me like you want. But in the right way. A man worthy of touching me, of knowing me. Someone who will take his time. This is worth waiting for, as desperate as you and I may feel for it, for the touch. Oh, be good to yourself, Julie Todd. I am proud to be your body. All in all, you have been very good to me and my purpose is to serve you, your true self, your highest purpose. We are on this journey together, and it is going to be increasingly amazing, joyful, free. I know it and you know it. Trust that, Julie. Trust me, please. The way is opening. The way is opening.

Journal Entry 2.25.14

To my beautiful, amazing body, When I think back over my life, my times of trouble and my times of healing, it has always been you that has been my vessel, my source of transformation. Despite the ways that I have ignored you, mistreated, overworked you, forced you into certain molds, judged you, you have been nothing but good to me. Compassionate. You have been my healer, the one who brings me back to my true self, my true home. You are the one God uses to heal and transform me and others – speaking through my hands, my back, my heart. You are the one who remains open to change, who gently and lovingly calls me to notice, shift, listen more deeply to the ways in which spirit calls me back to awareness, new life. Your intelligence, your intuition, your beauty, your resilience never cease to amaze me. You are a miracle and a miracle worker, I desire to bow to your wisdom. To give my mind to your understanding. I know that it is my analytic mind that has caused me to be distant from you. So I thank you for being patient with me. For always trying to send me messages the loving and kind way. But because I have not listened, sometimes you have to up the ante – anxiety, back pain.

I am trying to listen to you now. Listen completely and utterly to how you are calling me into this next stage of my life. I know you want me to do powerful works. I need for you to tell me which ways to go – my hands, my heart, my back. I will do my best to listen and listen. I want the distance between you and me, you and my mind, you and my ego, to close. To let love flow freely, fully in me and to others. I so desperately want to love you completely, to never hurt you again. To be obedient to what you are telling me. To let my deepest desire arise from you, and to surrender to it as good, as a desire that comes directly from God, that is God, that is God's own desire for me. How I love you, my body. How can I come to know and love you more, my body. Please accept how sorry I am for not listening and loving you. I want to be better about that. Accept my humble offering to listen more, to believe in you, what you offer and tell me, the way God is using you to be priestess to me.

I dedicate myself to you, with all my heart and soul, Julie

Like many cisgender women and gender-nonconforming people, I was taught to hate my body. I have written my body and myself many letters to talk myself out of this self-hatred.

Nothing Left to Give
(In Memory of Webb)
Journal Entry 7.23.14

[Sing] Amazing Grace 1ˢᵗ verse
His wife asked me to sing that first verse of Amazing Grace
Before I gave his eulogy
He always loved it when I sang (so freely)
He the immigrant Swede, so tall and lanky
Soft heart, he had always been so good to me
How I loved him and his wife both

But that morning before the memorial service,
You see,
While I was sitting at my vanity
Blow-drying my hair,
Weeping uncontrollably,
It dawned on me
"I can't do it."
I breathed. [Breathe in, breathe out]

"You have to stop crying."
[Breathe in, breathe out]
    "You have to stop crying."
    "You must sing. You must speak."
    "You have to stop crying."
[Breathe in, breathe out]
But I can't.
I can't stop crying.
And I realized
"I can't do this."
"I can't do this anymore."
"I have nothing left to give."
I am actually feeling resentful to give a man's funeral
A man I loved.
But I have nothing left to give.
Well running dry.
In that moment, I knew I could no longer be a pastor.

It's crazy, you see,
Following one who died on a tree
Giving all, the ultimate sacrifice
So others would have life
When there is no way to live up
To that one who would give up
Everything he had
And then I feel bad
When in fact, unlike Christ
I am human, not God
Even if I am divine
And now understand
That I must draw the line

I did dig deep
And sing that day
Underestimated the measure
Of the depth of the well,
It's a treasure
Sustained by a strength
From a God who takes pleasure

In pouring grace without limits
On we who have limits

I have limits
I cannot love and heal others
If I have nothing left to give
So ten years hence I am learning to live

The scene I describe in this piece happened in 2004. This was when I decided I had to leave pastoral ministry in the local church, which I did in 2005.

You Can't Put Constraints On the Soul

Guerrilla Society prompt: "My spirituality, my soul"
October 2014

My spirituality,
Gee.
In the company of Tim, Keyla, Rania, Junior, and Klinny.
Nothing less than the image of God in me
That IS me.
That spark of creativity
Born into mortality,
But existent eternally.
Deep alignment and connectivity
To life force energy
One speck in the Creator's panoply
One with the stardust and moonlight and every kind of tree
Bearing the DNA of both flowers and bees
And the salty taste of dark oceans deep.

All of us one, but no one like me
Awesome and limited in my particularity,
Earthbound, yes, descending from a family tree
But in my spirit and soul, yearning to be free.
Unbound from any social imaginary
All constraint or impossibility
Belief in utter transformativity
Working for the liberation of all creation
I want that to be my spiritual legacy

My spirituality
Discerning and intuiting moment to moment
The true nature of each being's ability
Awakening their vitality.
Encouraging in spiritual community
A mind-renewing desire for justice
Rather than a world of dull conformity.

My spirituality
Saying no to a society
That claims resistance to oppression
Is a form of impropriety
In a culture born of imperialism, drunk on materialism
I cling to my sobriety
Simplicity is a guide to me
Spiritual identity
Bedrock integrity
Soul transparency
Never seeking to hide nor flee.

My spirituality
Sees each soul in its beauty and plurality
Never reducing any one
To the image of me.
I regard each one in their own manifestation
Of concrete divinity.
Each one clearly a majesty
At the same time a profound mystery
Never truly known by me.

I bow in the humility
Of what it means to be human, just to BE.

On bended knee
I pray
To see thee more clearly
Love thee more dearly
Follow thee more nearly[1]
Creator within me
The image you placed internally
Yes, I am worthy
Softly and tenderly you call me,
Dwelling in my body,
"Julie."

After I moved back to Lawrence, I began volunteering with a writing group at Movement City, an after-school program. This writing group spun off on its own and called itself the Guerrilla Society (GS). We met weekly to write and performed occasionally. It was a remarkable group of shining stars and brilliant minds, five of whom I name at the beginning of the piece because they were sitting at the table when this poem came. All of the members of GS are cherished humans in my life. When I read this piece aloud back to the group immediately after writing it, Tim remarked, "You can't put constraints on the soul." So that is what I titled this.

---

[1] "To see thee more clearly, love thee more dearly, follow thee more nearly," are lyrics from the song "Day by Day," from the musical *Godspell*, which I grew up listening to.

RED BELL BOTTOM JEANS
Sometime in 2014

I am from North Andover, Mass
That's right next door here to Lawrence, yes
I moved there from Lynn
The city of sin

In the third grade
On the first day of school
In my new town
On the playground
Trying to be cool
A few girls circled round
You know how girls can be cruel

They pointed at my red bell bottom jeans
And laughed
"Lynn, Lynn, City of Sin
Never Go Out the way you came in."

Mean-girl voices high-pitched, whiny and thin
Their words pricked like a pin

And then one asked me, nasty, but kind of mellow
"I don't know, but are you from, like, the ghetto?"
Not expecting an answer, though it was no
I realized there was something about those
Red bell bottom jeans that seemed to show
That I was poor, and for the gatekeepers of popularity
Poor was a "do not pass go"

I don't even know
If those chicks were rich
But I know they thought
I had not a stitch
They thought I was poor
And poor was bad
And all of a sudden
I was not glad
To have moved from the city
Where sure the streets were gritty
To the place of the rolling hills
I did not appreciate their pity
Because to me, there was nothing wrong
Nothing wrong at all
With Sin City

Here I must stop for a bit
Let me just state plainly for the record
That those red bell bottom jeans were THE SHIT

And from that time forward
In my eight-year-old mind
I vowed never, ever
To be so unkind
To never ever be like those snotty rich kids
From that suburban town
Who think when they find
A poor kid

Or any semblance of difference from them
That they can put that one down
And to this day when I think of the suburbs
I frown
At those who wear wealth and conformity
Like a fine evening gown

So I promised to never, ever
Be like them those asses
North Andover tried to beat out of me
My roots in the working classes
And they may have succeeded
But yet as time passes
I see in myself a hard-scrabble working-class attitude
That my soul has always heeded
That I like to think was based on the gospel message of Jesus
Who claimed the poor and those who don't belong
Are the ones who are most valued and needed

So I call upon my immigrant ancestors
From the working masses
My Lithuanian grandparents
The Dougwillos,
Some of whom were boxers, scrappy super bad-asses
Who we always thought were Polish
But who only called themselves that
So as to pass
Because the only thing worse than being Polish
Was being Lithuanian
Who were thought to be crass.

The Todds from Lawrence who descended from the Mayflower
Which my grandfather thought was a source of great power
My Irish great-grandparents, the Averills and the Murphys
Devout Catholics who swore like truck drivers and read teacup leaves
My farming ancestors from rural Tennessee
Who tilled the fields and spoke German
And who lived on the land sustainably

I call these ancestors into my life
To stand with that girl in the third grade
In her moment of class-based strife
With her fresh, red bell bottom jeans
Who questioned for the rest of her life
The poverty and injustice which in this country is rife
Who asked
Why is there a gap between the rich and the poor
Why your money makes you good
And the appearance of poverty closes the door
To your heart
And makes poor people bad.
Because that is some shit
That is backwards and hateful
It makes me so sad, and mad

I'll take my dope, red bell bottom jeans
Over your prejudice
And snobbish conventionality
Any day of the week
And claim within me this hard-nose working-class streak

I don't hate North Andover, despite its cliques
It didn't make me clannish
I loved where I grew up
The trees, forests, lake and winding roads
In which my soul vanished
And one of the greatest things it gave me
North Andover schools taught me to speak Spanish

Que me ayuda mucho en esta ciudad
When I say I'm from here, I feel proud
Because yeah, I live in Law-Town now
And so, North Andover,
At your class-based high-brow
I take verbal aim
Ka-pow!

Psalm 51 Rewrite
Journal Entry 3.5.15

Have mercy on me, O God
According to your steadfast love
According to your abundant mercy
Help me to let go of
All that does not serve –
      Me, you and others
Wash me thoroughly from all the broken patterns of my life
And cleanse me of my foolish resentments
For I know the ways in which I have failed to be faithful
The ways I have deluded myself and others are ever before me
In the end, all of these things only cause me
      to be apart from you, O God,
      and others
So I dishonor the divine within myself and others
I waste the power you have given me for good
So that each time I come before you
To confess what I have done and not done

The places where you judge and I need to repent become clear
Indeed, some of these patterns of resistance to your love –
        To receiving it and sharing it –
Seem present in me since the earliest times I can remember
You desire truth in the inward being
Therefore, teach me wisdom in my secret heart
Purge me through surrender, that I might be
        clear of the residue of my many agendas
Wash me of the transgressions of ego that my body, mind, and spirit
        might be refreshed to serve
With joy and gladness
Let this feeling of being sick and tired of the cold, weary world pass away
So that my connection with your spirit might become apparent to all
Create in me a clean heart, O God,
And put a new and a right spirit within me.
I have never felt apart from you
And I ask that it may never be so.
But restore in me the joy of serving
And sustain in me a willing spirit
Then I will teach others about healing
So that they might understand the power of your divine love
Deliver me from any acts that might cause harm to another
O God of Abundant Grace,
And let who you are shine through me clearly
In word and deed.
O God, open my lips
In ways that express the fullness of life
That is available to all
For you have no delight in the ways we sacrifice our lives
        to no good purpose
The sacrifice that is acceptable to God
Is a vulnerable spirit that is open to your leading
A humble heart and a willingness to change and serve, you will not reject
You desire for us to work for our own highest good
        and the highest good of all
You urge us to rebuild the bonds of community
        in the places we live and work
When we work for justice and love in this world you take great delight

The work of hands, heart, and healing
that we lay on the altar
that is your world
Is your utmost calling on our lives.

Ode to SNIRT
3.19.15

My new most/least favorite word:
SNIRT
(SNow-dIRT)

Oh, Snirt, how I want to hate you so much.
Everywhere I look,
there you are.
Piles of your ugliness.
Yuck. Blech. Blargh. Spht. Ugh.
I wish you would just:
Go. Away.

Reminders of the winter from hell
2 tows, 4 parking tickets, a smashed side mirror
You are gross and ugly and full of garbage we have left behind

Oh, Snirt, how I want to hate you so much.
But somehow, I just can't.
I stand outside and look at you
as I stand on the edge of this spring
& there is something about you
that reminds me – of me.

Piles of hard, cold dirt that are the residues
from the hard seasons of my life;
full of the garbage that I have thrown on top
in between the occasional angry flurries of emotion.
I look at the residue of long-past storms of resentment and fear.
I see the frozen-solidness of that which needs to be let go,
and I wish it would all just melt away,
FASTER.

The sunny-but-still-cold days
Remind me
that learning to live with the cold ugly hard spots
takes time.

Some days of melting emotions flow down fast
like their own side streets
And other days the hard piles linger,
melt a little
eke out on sidewalks,
freeze again.
& make it hard to move forward
as easily & quickly as I'd like to
without slipping
or falling
and hurting myself

Oh, Snirt, how I want to hate you so much
But underneath your hard surface
your apparent ugly & hard cold
you continue to be a warm blanket
for the earth.
Slowly nourishing her soil

with your water
as the beautiful new, green growth
mystery and magic yet unknown
deep within
wants to burst forth
blossom
into flowers
with joy, promise
for a new future

& so your slow melt is perfection

& so the slow melt of my imperfections is also perfection.

For Everything
there is a season

Oh, Snirt, how I want to hate you so much
But I can't. And I don't.
You take your time
& I'll take mine.

I heard the word "snirt" used for the first time by Natalie, an herbal teacher in the Boston School of Herbal Studies. The day I heard it, I went home and wrote this.

The Foolishness of Love

The Common Sage
Writing Prompt by Jennifer Hilton
4.1.15 (April Fools Day)

I have been foolish, yes
I have been foolish
I have loved when I knew better
I have given my heart in places
Where I knew it would be broken
I have poured my love into another's cup
Knowing that love would never be returned
To make my cup full
I have believed in other's goodness
And refreshed my forgiveness
Time and time again
And against all evidence.
I have found myself so weak
From disappointment and grief
That I have thought I will never love again

Yes, I have been foolish
But I have heard it said
That God chooses the foolish
To shame the wise
God chooses the weak
To shame the strong
So I love that I am weak
For people's goodness
I love that I am foolishly forgiving
I love that even as I have given more than
Perhaps I should have
That my capacity to love has no end
I am deep with love for people
And if it is the most foolish thing
I could possibly be or do
Then I would be and do no other
Because to love much is to live much
To love foolishly
Is to live fully.

I moved to Lawrence, MA, from Colorado in the fall of 2013. A local bookstore-café called El Taller had recently opened. El Taller was and is a gathering place for local creatives of all kinds, providing spaces for writing, conversation, education, and performance. Many of the people I first met when I returned to Lawrence, I met at El Taller. Many had been participants in the Andover Bread Loaf (ABL) writing workshops and the Bread Loaf Teacher Network, extensions of the Bread Loaf School of English in Vermont. The ABL method is primarily writing-prompt based free-writing. The writing prompts themselves can be almost anything: questions, ideas, art, performance, presentations, conversation. Both the Guerrilla Society and The Common Sage writing groups I was part of were descendants of ABL participants.

Do I Have a Poem In Me Today?
Journal Entry
4.15.15

Do I have a poem in me today?
Some days I just seem to have a poem in me
And it comes tumbling out
All rough and ready for the world
Inspired
And like, I don't even know
Where it came from
And then other days
Nothing.
Nothing. Nothing. Nothing.
And yet on those days when there seems to be nothing
Deep down I know there's something
Waiting
Like an apple
To ripen
And be picked from a tree

Or when it is so ripe
It just falls to the ground
From its own weight and readiness
And like an apple picked too soon
That is too hard and tart to eat
A poem sometimes needs its moment
        Of ripeness
Some things simply should not be forced
Do I have a poem in me today?
Definitely.
Is she ready?
I trust her to let me know
So then waiting for a poem
Is akin to living life
That tender balance of waiting
Then knowing when the time is right
Letting life flow
The creative juices
Knowing when to pick the fruits on the tree of life
When they are just right
Ripe and sweet
For the harvest

I dare you
Original 4.26.15

I dare you
No, I dare me
to be as creative
as our souls call us to be

I dare you,
No, I dare me
to break the bonds of
dull, institutionalized conformity

to believe
that deep within
lies a well
of endless possibility

I dare you,
No, I dare me
to reject rampant individualism,
captain of this ship called savage capitalism
Abandon Ship!
I declare, "Mutiny!"
Let us walk the plank to the edges of our isolation
And dive into the raging waters of community

I dare you,
No, I dare me
to embrace the horrible magic
we call vulnerability
where my fear, my weakness
my poverty, my depravity
shared with you
and yours with me
becomes the fertile ground
of a newly imagined humanity

I dare you,
No, I dare me
to break
the hard, dark ground
of oppression & brutality
admit thoroughly
our investment
in a domination mentality
the spaces we occupy within
the male, white, able-bodied
complex of heteropatriarchal
christian superiority

Go ahead,
I dare you
Confess that to me

Go ahead,
I dare you,

No, I dare me
Because if we can't be honest about our history
about how my people killed & enslaved your people
& so how now you and your people, how you may actually hate me
if we can't fight and play
in that down and dirty reality

Crack open through truth-telling
the real barriers
the real barriers to harmony
the real barriers to mining
our inner terrains for all of their
richness and beauty

If our creativity can't help us to do that
Then, so what? Who cares?
Who are we?

I dare you
No, I dare me
to embrace The One in whose image we are made
The Author of All Creativity
Before whom
& Before You
I stand in All Humility
Begging
Daring we

Be no longer satisfied
with comfort, complacency, complicity
with our very own destruction
& the destruction of the earth
whose essence is the very ground of our connectivity

So with every breath and every cell and every step and every word and
every action
Let us resist our captivity
People, let's get free

I dare you
No, I dare me
I dare we
The only way out –
is through
the gift of Our Creator
to the human personality
is
Our Creativity

I think this is the only piece I ever tried to write for performance with the Guerrilla Society. It originated in the writing prompt "truth or dare."

Vulnerability
The Common Sage
Writing Prompt by Theresa Limes
5.6.15

I think sometimes
I would rather die
Than expose them to you
My vulnerabilities
I don't want you to see me weak
See me afraid
See me cry
See me broken
I suppose, in a sense
That you, anyone
Would truly
SEE ME.
See how alone I feel most days
How much I fear losing my parents
I'm afraid you will find out

I am a big fake
That I question myself
That I'm not as smart as I seem
That I do not actually have my shit together
That I'm an alcoholic
That I hate my body
That I often resent being helpful to others
That I had an affair with a married man.
That the thought of you knowing me
Really seeing me fully
As a whole and wholly real human
Might cause you to think less of me
Deride me
Reject me
And, as I said
I already feel alone enough most days.
So I pretend.
But I pretended so much in my life
It took too much energy.
I found myself
Less and less able to find myself
And I burned out
I burned down
And broke into a thousand pieces
And picking up
All the sharp shards of myself
Lying around on the floor
And holding them out to people and saying,
"Help."
"I'm going to need some help putting myself
Back together again."
These small steps into the
Deep dark terrain of vulnerability,
Moments that made me
        Want to puke
        And still do,
Began the process of healing
        Of connecting
With other humans, who

Just like me –
Feel lonely most days
Are tired
Are literally sick and tired
Of being people we are not
Of never feeling safe
To open and share their hearts
Their souls
To the painful realities of life

Without the cracks in the walls
There is no way for the light to get in

Still Can't Fucking Write

The Common Sage
Writing Prompt by Mary Guerrero:
Why doesn't the power of writing & power of coming together happen in schools? How is the yearning for education in such contrast to how much people hate school?
5.27.15

The stupidest thing about it
The stupidest fucking whole thing about it
Is that I still think, "I can't write."
I swear I am telling you the truth when I tell you
I don't think I'm a good writer
I don't know when it started
Perhaps in the 3rd grade
when I moved from the gritty city of Lynn
to the suburbs of North Andover
and the cruel girls on the playground
made fun of my red bell bottom jeans
which were, mind you
the absolute shit

But by their jeers
I knew they thought I was poor
and in so many ways, not enough
Or maybe it was in middle school when they forced you to learn to write
sentence DIAGRAM things with those stupid straight
lines that broke off for verbs & objects & participles
and made absolutely no sense
Or maybe it was the 11th grade
in that same snob-ass N. Andover suburb
Honors English class, mind you
when I poured my heart out in a love poem
based on the picture of a bridge
over dry land
          that went to nowhere
And my teacher
Gave Me an F and said,
"Rewrite, too sentimental."
Or maybe it was in the first semester
of my Master's degree, mind you
When I wrote my first paper
for early christian history and
the professor ripped it to red pen shreds
and wrote at the end,
"Not worth a grade, Julie,
This is graduate school."
And now I sit here in this chair
with my fucking Ph.D., mind you
and still have this feeling that
I can't write
          I'm not a good writer
WHAT. THE. FUCK.
They don't want us to write with our hearts
They want us to be consumers, not
          creators
Conformers, not resisters
They want us to be them – bound
not ourselves – free
They want us docile capitalists
Not passion-filled rebels

Two weeks ago Theresa told me that I
        write like Niagara Falls
In torrents
        that Pour out of my pen
wide full white water crashing rivers
that flow out of my pen in a
direction and I have no idea
where I'm headed
and I'm writing so fast to try and
keep up with my thoughts
that I haven't even thought yet
and then something comes out
and I barely know what I said
and then I take a big breath
and I read it to the group
and everyone looks at me, like,
"WHOA, what the fuck, Julie,"
but this time it's what the fuck
in a good way and it
appears that I have connected
with others' hearts & minds &
I say to every single public school
teacher in that snot-ass public school
system & high brow higher ed program

FUCK YOU
I can write

If I became blind
The Common Sage Writing Prompt
6.4.2015

I had a professor once
she taught Christian worship
in the seminary I attended
and she asked us what it would be like
to worship God if you could not see
And all of us, so invested as we were
in the written word
and the look of the sanctuary
and seeing the symbols
we could not imagine
And she asked us to consider the
      inner knowing
      the inner sense
      the inner perception
That is of God
That is God

That which simply knows when
it is in the presence of the divine
without cognition
That which smells
That which hears
That which touches, tastes
That which, ultimately FEELS.
Not the mind so much as the HEART.
I do not know if my professor was blind
from birth or if she became blind
But one day, for some reason I
can't remember
She went around the room and told each
one of us students how she imagined
us in her inner knowing
And she told me that I was a willow tree
          Tall & old
          majestic & wise
          That I had a strength & beauty
          and a solid sadness
          that draped over others
          as a protection
And I wondered how she knew this
How she imagined this, saw this
And saw me
Truly saw me
Though she could not see
All I can say is that would it be me
I would hope for that sense
          of inner knowing
          that guidance & perception
          that is of God
          that is God
that I would trust to guide & lead me
the thing is
I know that I have that knowing
and I do see
(but do not yet trust)

What Makes Me Weary?

The Common Sage
Alan Núñez Writing prompt: What Makes You Weary?
(after singing Langston Hughes' *Weary Blues*)
7.1.2015

Weary.
Wicked fucking weary.
Weary of the gap
between the way things are
& the way things
could be.
Weary of people who won't stand
in that gap.
Weary of white liberals
who speak the language of justice
but who don't do jack shit.
Weary of apathy
& "nothing will ever change."
Weary of

"thank you for speaking, Julie, I don't have the courage."
Weary of black bodies shot dead
on streets
& in churches.
Weary of burning churches.
Weary of racist culture
that speaks the language of liberty and justice for all,
but which lives in the denial of genocide, slavery, and their legacies.
Weary of white liberals
who think racism is the problem of
"those people,"
white supremacists,
the extreme ones.
Weary of those who do not understand
the systems and structures of racism
that pervade our every move.
Weary of educating the ignorant.
Weary of educating my own people.
Weary of remembering that it is my task as a white person
to work with my own people.
Weary of church people
who think they are saviors.
Weary of Christian individualism.
Weary of people who think –
      Disruption
      Destruction
      Disclosing the Truth –
who think that's the problem.
Weary of people who think
black people are the problem
brown people are the problem.
Weary of #AllLivesMatter.
Weary of calls for cheap unity and reconciliation.
Weary of the fear of difference.
Weary of turn the other cheek as a tool of pacification.
Weary of wanting justice.
Weary of racism.
Weary of calls for "Peace, peace, where there is no peace."
Weary of mass incarceration of brown bodies.

Weary of profits over people.
Weary of party politics.
Weary of being dismissed for my radical ideals.
Weary of people telling me
"that's just not practical, Julie"
"face reality, Julie."
(No, fuck you, you face reality.)
Weary of never feeling like
Love is something more than
a cheap embrace
or sentimentality
or being nice.
Weary that no one sees revolution as a form of love.
Weary that no one sees struggle as a form of spiritual practice.

The Need to Breathe
(I CAN'T BREATHE, HE SAID)
Andover Bread Loaf Summer Program
Student-Teacher Joint Workshop
Facilitated by Erwin Thomas on Change
Written after the workshop 7.11.15

Erwin came to speak to youth about change,
writing about change
About changing his mind about change
or becoming wise about change
becoming comfortable with
being uncomfortable with change
Because whether you accept change
resist change
you will become uncomfortable
with change
our relationship to the only thing that is
CHANGE
how change happens

how our views on change
CHANGE
Change comes not how you speak, he said
change laughs at us, he said
embrace the patience that
comes with change, he said
CHANGE – CLAP, CLAP, CLAP he said
CHANGE – CLAP, CLAP, CLAP he said
CHANGE, he SAID –

BREATHE, he said
BREATHE, he said
BREATHE all the way down to your belly, he said
BREATHE
               Relax, he said
Keep breathing
       try to relax into change
       try to be present with change
       flow with the change
       watch the change
       observe the change
       WITHOUT FEAR, he said

DON'T FORGET to
       BREATHE
Because when we stop breathing, he said
We DIE, he said.

Because when we stop breathing, he said
We DIE, he said.

I CAN'T BREATHE, HE SAID
I CAN'T BREATHE, HE SAID
I CAN'T BREATHE, HE SAID
I CAN'T BREATHE, HE SAID
I CAN'T BREATHE, HE SAID
I CAN'T BREATHE, HE SAID
I CAN'T BREATHE, HE SAID
I CAN'T BREATHE, HE SAID

I CAN'T BREATHE, HE SAID
I CAN'T BREATHE, HE SAID
I CAN'T BREATHE, HE SAID

Breathe, he said.
Breathe, he said
If you stop breathing, you die, he said
once you stop breathing, you can't change
So change
Breathe, he said

Smoking will kill you, they say
fill your lungs with cancer
drown you with your own fluid, they say
so you can't breathe, they say
But selling loose cigarettes
will kill you even faster than cancer, it seems
chokeholds will kill you faster than drowning, it seems
cops with impunity & no accountability
        kill faster than you can say police brutality, it seems

I CAN'T BREATHE, HE SAID
I CAN'T BREATHE, HE SAID
I CAN'T BREATHE, HE SAID
I CAN'T BREATHE, HE SAID
I CAN'T BREATHE, HE SAID
I CAN'T BREATHE, HE SAID
I CAN'T BREATHE, HE SAID
I CAN'T BREATHE, HE SAID
I CAN'T BREATHE, HE SAID
I CAN'T BREATHE, HE SAID
I CAN'T BREATHE, HE SAID
BREATHE, HE SAID

My moon sister, she says
The more you breathe the more you heal, she says
The more you breathe the more you heal, she says
Breathe all the way down to the belly, she says
Breathe all the way down to the belly, she says

Like, Erwin, she says
Soften the Belly, she says
Soften the Belly, she says
Soften the gaze, they say
Soften the gaze, they say
(soften)

BUT I DON'T WANT TO SOFTEN
(soften)
BUT I DON'T WANT TO SOFTEN
(soften)
BUT I DON'T WANT TO SOFTEN
(soften)
Because people can't breathe, you see
PEOPLE CAN'T BREATHE, you see
PEOPLE CAN'T BREATHE, you see
PEOPLE CAN'T BREATHE, you see
PEOPLE CAN'T BREATHE
And I don't want to be soft on cops
WHEN THEY ARE TOUGH ON CRIME
(soften)
And I like my edges hard
When facing down monsters
And I like my wolverine claws out
when you're attacking my people
And I ain't gonna go all soft for
Your rhetoric about freedom & peace
And you could not pay me one million dollars
to turn MY FUCK YOUs into Please & Thank-yous
My heat is my fire
and if you can't take the heat
get the hell out of the kitchen
Because it is burning up in here
and you closed and bolted the doors
And the smoke is so THICK
that PEOPLE ARE CHOKING
AND SCREAMING
        IN WHISPERS (and I don't want to go soft)
WE CAN'T BREATHE

WE CAN'T BREATHE
WE CAN'T BREATHE
WE CAN'T BREATHE
WE CAN'T BREATHE
WE CAN'T BREATHE
WE CAN'T BREATHE
WE CAN'T BREATHE
WE CAN'T BREATHE
WE CAN'T BREATHE
WE CAN'T BREATHE
WE CAN'T BREATHE

Breathe.
The more you breathe the more you heal
BREATHE
The more you breathe the more you heal
HEALING requires CHANGE
HEALING requires CHANGE
HEALING requires CHANGE
     And no one can heal for us
     Only we can heal ourselves
     and healing is hard
     because healing requires change
AND LIFE IS HARD ENOUGH and who has time for change
AND LIFE IS HARD ENOUGH and who has energy for change

BREATHE, HE SAID
BREATHE, HE SAID
BREATHE, HE SAID
BREATHE

On July 17, 2014, Mr. Eric Garner said, "I can't breathe" eleven times, while a New York City police officer held him face-down on a sidewalk in a choke-hold, resulting in Garner's death. Mr. Garner was accosted by the police ostensibly for selling loose cigarettes on the streets.

On Church Unity
7.20.2015

Sometimes
the word unity
slips off the tongue
like a bad french kiss
from a teenage lover
leaving me feeling
sticky and gross.

Sometimes
the word unity
tastes like
nasty cough medicine
my mother made me take
from a stainless steel spoon
its cherry "sweetness"
making me gag.

Sometimes
the word unity
looms like a jackhammer
held by a laborer
in the idle position
next to a crumbling urban sidewalk
the jackhammer mocking:
"hold it together, hold it together."

Sometimes unity
masquerades
as *ekklesia*
body parts working harmoniously,
hands and feet needing each other
when injustice like gangrene
untreated and festering
implies an impending amputation.

Sometimes unity
masquerades
as ideology
holding fast to theological abstractions
the comfort of inaction
for those who refuse
to make a clear-cut choice
for justice.

Sometimes unity
masquerades
as Christ himself
caught between
no more stone-throwing
& cursing a courageous woman
comparing her to a dog
who begs for scraps
she does not deserve.

A main argument against removing all anti-gay language from The Book of Discipline of The United Methodist Church *or taking a prophetic word-and-deed stand of any kind for full justice and inclusion of* LGBTQ+ *folks is that such actions are alienating and would split* The United Methodist Church. *Published on Love Prevails' website and social media: https://loveprevailsumc.com/2015/07/20/on-church-unity/.*

Fearfully Wonderfully
Journal Entry 7.31.2015

I am fearfully & wonderfully made
Dropped into this universe
on some crazy-ass time-space continuum
that I do not pretend to understand
just in order to be myself
like my only purpose in life
is to figure out just how fabulous I am
and to share that with others
so they can also know
how beautiful they are
we all are.
So just like God dropped me on
This crazy earth
it seems finally come time
to drop now into myself
fully commit
to myself

to being no one else but me
humble, in relation to others
but free
how interconnection
and interdependence
how justice
       love &
       abundance
need me
to be me
and not what others think I should be
       or want me to be
       or wish I was
       but that I must be, wholly,
            who God created me to be
in order for all of us to flourish.
this is less about ego, though
and more,
       or all
       about love
           for myself
           others
           creation

If that flower is not fully itself
       then I am less
Thing is, that flower
           ONLY KNOWS
how to be itself
       even when what is around it
       a sometimes toxic environment
       might prevent its fullness
it still lives, only to be itself
in the world
in relationship to everything around it
without judgment

And so, is the flower less when I am not fully myself?
No, the flower, she is fully herself, my role model.

How Queer
Journal entry 7.31.2015

How Queer
how queer
for people to see me
(or not)
to look at me
and wonder
(or not)
who is she
what is she
who are they
how are they
who is he
what is he
is he queer
is she gay
are they, um… you know…
how queer.

people
have always wondered
never known
had to ask
never asked
always assumed
because don't ask
don't tell
how queer
this not asking
this not telling
in this world obsessed
with identification
how queer.
Jesus Christ asked:
"Who do you say that I am?"
not because
he didn't know himself
but to expose
false impressions
preconceived ideas
false categories
who people
thought he was
how he was
but no
he was, something else
behold: he was something altogether new
unimagined
how queer

The High of Being Mighty

Hiroshima Day 70th anniversary
8.6.2015

What always
stays in my mind
are the stone steps
that
captured
a human image.
The white-hot light
from an atomic blast
so bright,
it cast a shadow;
so hard,
it burned, forever
Into stone
the apparition of a human.
Whose fleshly form
disappeared.

Gone.
The heat.
The light.
The force of blast.
Utterly.
Obliterating.
Matter.
All that is left,
Shadow.

August 6, 1945
The U.S. (us) dropped
the first atomic bomb
on humanity.

As many times, dozens
as I walked through
The Peace Museum
In Hiroshima, Japan
I simply
Could not
Take.
It.
In.
The horror of that day
only overshadowed
by the fact:
Three days later,
we did it
Again.

Nagasaki, Japan
August 9, 1945
Second atomic bomb
Different kind of bomb this time
(why? ask yourself, Why?)

Hundreds of Thousands of Japanese dead.

Experimentation with
the obliteration
of matter;
Of life.
Of life that does not matter.
Experimentation with power
power to destroy life
life that does not matter;
The High
of being mighty.
The High of Being Mighty.
The high
of feeling higher
more powerful
than another/s.
U.S. (us) life:
my power
my money
Matters
More
Than Yours.
Than all other life.

To take in the atomic bombs
To really stop.
Go ahead,
Stop. & try to take it in.
The atomic bomb dropped on two major cities
We did that.

To really take it in,
to open one's spirit
for even some few moments
to disallow the refusal
to see
to be aware
& let the spirit of destruction
touch our
Deepest collective shadow

is to know
& #neveragain deny
that our legacy
U.S. (us)
is the obliteration of matter.
& in this country
it has always been the case
that some lives matter
More
than others.

To let that truthfulness touch
each of us;
deeply acknowledge
our own capacity
to obliterate matter.
To crave
The High of Being Mighty
Be it
Mighty White
Mighty Male
Mighty American
Mighty Straight
Mighty Christian
Mighty Human.
Our belief
in our mighty right
to own
to destroy
Casts shadows.
Long, hard shadows that endure;
that turn life into stone.

& so to resist
to refuse The
High of Being Mighty
may be our first step

towards the kind of Light
that casts
more than shadows.

#blacklivesmatter

I lived in Hiroshima, Japan from 1991–1993.

Influence
The Common Sage Prompt:
Someone who influenced me making right choices
10.14.2015

She said to me:
"I don't know if you are an alcoholic or not,
but I know that, if you are
and you go home tomorrow
and you drink,
you will die.
Maybe not tomorrow,
or the next day,
or next week,
or next month.
But if you really have a problem
and you go home
and drink tomorrow
eventually, it will kill you."
That's what she said.

That was May 9th, 2001
The next day, I left
and I never saw her again
I spoke to her once
she called me
like she said she would
"sometime, one day"
to ask me
if I had ever had a drink.
And when she called me
sometime during that next year
I told her I had not had a drink
And I hadn't
And to this day,
I still haven't
over (18) years later.

I only knew her
        Ginny was her name
        for 8 days
        8 short days
The first day I met her
She told me she believed in miracles
I thought that sounded a little stupid
In the end, she said
        "see, you are a miracle"
Her words
influenced me
for a lifetime
Every moment since then
every choice I have made
has stemmed from that one choice I made
that next day
and then the next
and the next
to not drink
I am amazed that one person
for one short period of time
could have such a profound influence

on every other choice
I have ever made
All choices that led to my health
    my freedom
    in fact
    the choice
    that gives me the ability
    every day
    to choose life, over death
Thank you, Ginny
    You were a miracle, too
    and I owe you my life.

Ginny was a Sister of Notre Dame and my spiritual director on a silent retreat at the Gonzaga Eastern Point Retreat House in Gloucester, MA.

DONE WITH TOXIC BULLSHIT
(on my parasite cleanse)
Journal entry 2.10.2016

Clearing out space
re-establishing patterns of health
the parasite cleanse was, in part, a metaphor
for clearing out
that which we easily co-exist with
sometimes that we do not even know is there
they prefer to hide
they are not malevolent
these old friends
robbing us of basic nourishment
like many beings we let live inside us
the ideas, thoughts, patterns of relating
co-existing, even surviving
that take, take,
take our fundamental energy
and we let them

because, well
that's just how it is
how did I get parasites
I don't know
though I have theories
it's like a lot of things
that live inside me
that I don't know how they got there
like
When did I start lying to myself?
When did I learn it is better to be strong than to be vulnerable?
When did I begin storing resentments instead of letting them go?
When did self-doubt creep in?
When did I start ignoring my pain?
Where did I learn that taking care of others
was more important than taking care of myself?
Where did I begin not listening to my inner voice?
When did my hatred of my body creep in?
Like the parasites,
I don't really know how all those things got there
FOR THAT MATTER
When was the exact point that I learned
white people were better than black & brown people?
When was the first time a man
degraded or diminished me for being female?
When did it dawn on me that my class status & education
gave me power over others?
Where do these things begin?
and how did I get parasites?
I do not know
but I can tell you this
I had so many parasites on my insides
that I had to do that cleanse twice
So for two months
I was on the bathroom floor
Looking inside my toilet,
digging around with a hanger & a spoon
and I realized
I had accumulated a lot of toxic bullshit

that waste product resulting
from the consumption of poisons
that I can't even recall swallowing,
      that garbage we call food
      that is the diet of America
      everything from Sour Patch Kids
            to Taco Hell
            to how bad he did me
            to white supremacy
and the longer you let that toxic brew
      sit on your insides
      it will take you over

So I am
literally
letting all that shit go
I have begun the process of making space
Inside Me
For Health
For Wholeness
Re-establishing patterns of being
That do not include
Swallowing
      that which does not serve
      that which does not serve me
      that which does not serve us

In 2016, I did an apprenticeship with an herbalist who was an expert in the herbal treatment of Lyme disease. His protocol recommended treating Lyme by addressing the presence of parasites in the digestive tract. Although I was never diagnosed with Lyme disease, because I had some of the identified symptoms of parasites and the herbal protocol could not harm me, I did the cleanse. It turned out I had a lot of parasites. I have written extensively about the experience of the parasite cleanse elsewhere, with pictures of my poop and everything. The essay was too long to include in this book, but if you are interested, you may ask me to send you a copy.

Lies & Apple Pies

Guerrilla Society writing prompt:
Why is this country so fucked up?
11.10.16 (after the presidential election)

Why is this country so fucked up?
It's the lies.

The lies
All-American as apple pies
warmed in an oven
whose temperature was set to genocide
with a big scoop of vanilla ice cream on top
its creamy, white-white-whiteness
melting down the sides
Oh, how we love the sickly sweetness of this pie

This melting pot that tries
To reduce the horrors of history
To break them down to a size
Most fit for the consumption

Of the stomachs
Whose bodies are daily clad in suits & ties
Whose own mouths speak falsehoods
They force us to swallow
Things we were taught to memorize
The pledge of allegiance
Drilled into the pint-sized
A poisonous brew
Of schooling and religion
That fills us up inside.

They say, "you are only as sick as your secrets"
And from the soles of our feet to the top of our head
We are sick.

Sick with lies
All-American as apple pies
Overindulging, full to nauseous
Of the sickening white sweetness
Melting down the sides
Our stomachs ache
Our systems break
From trying to metabolize
The reality of robbery into the deceit of discovery
Death and enslavement into freedom and democracy
No
these are lies
That we have glamorized
Then globalized.

And because they are not true

And because they are not true
They will lead to our demise
Because a house built on shifting sand
will dematerialize

As for me,
I no longer seek to be anesthetized

From truth
From the reality of the underside
This country's foundation
in white supremacy
whose purpose
was and is to terrorize and dehumanize
In order to capitalize
To gain power and profit
Off the labor and the backs
Of the very people
We demonize

No more distance
that being white gives me
From my ability to empathize
With honesty, pain, and struggle
and with every effort
of everyday people to resist
to bring the powerful down to size
to be unafraid to criticize
the mighty U.S.A.
for whose pledge of allegiance
and star-spangled banner
I Do Not Rise

But instead

I Rise
Together with those who raise their battle cries
In streets and on stages and in classrooms
People who bring their wounded souls and real problems
from their communities,
people willing to analyze.

And the people who actually give a shit
And do something about it
Who have the courage to realize
That their personal struggles

And conditions of their communities
must be politicized.

And by politicized
I do not mean voting
Though of course, please, do
Because I can't stand people who rationalize
Inaction
And "the system will never change so why bother"
They love it when we believe those lies

What I mean by politicize
Is "of the people, by the people, for the people"
People who are willing to revolutionize
First, Our minds
Take every damn thing we thought was true
and turn our thoughts like a leaf
To the sun
By whose light the darkness of the lies
Is photosynthesized
That is, to harness the energy
Of the truth that shines
transforms poisonous dioxides
Captivating the energy within each of us
An energy which
When shared collectively together
In a poem or a protest
Allows for life itself to be catalyzed

I love apple pies
And I will keep eating them
But I will not swallow your
Plate of warm, white lies
Their sweetness no longer tempts me
Not even that scoop of sweet, white ice cream melting down the sides
So don't even try

Little Toes
(bunion surgery sucks)
Journal Entry 2.21.2017

My swollen, stagnant little toe
I love you and
I'm sorry for what I put you thru
historically
all those bad shoes
and this surgery.
and I thank you
and both you magical feet
and all you toes
for holding me up
so well
so strong
for all these years.
little swollen toe
you are keeping me honest
and by honest

I mean vulnerable
not letting me
move forward
too fast, too far
making me string out
this time of slow
and restoration
a little
longer
it is amazing what
power a small part
of the body has.
And I wonder if you are not holding
onto, holding onto
more than your share
of my stagnant energy
everything that wants to
drain
out of my body right now
a fair bit of energetic
garbage.
You may be catching it all.
Together let us work on
releasing the stuck stuff
that which has protected us
until now
served its purpose
but we are ready
for it to leave.
Thank you for holding
so much for me
like all of my yuck
is right there
and you are holding it
just like you have held me up
for years.

The Thing [I Thought]
I Was Most Afraid to Write About
Original April 2017; Rewrite July 2019

The spoken word artist and author Elizabeth Acevedo came
to perform at El Taller in Lawrence, MA. In an audience Q&A, she
said, "Write about the thing that you are most afraid to write about."
I often asked myself what that might be. Eventually, I wrote about
the thing I thought I was most afraid to write about. It turned out
that it wasn't that hard to write. It felt good to name the difficulties
of an earlier time in my life. The first draft was nearly ten full pages
of poetry. The claiming and communicating was a release of fear and
shame. I intended to include that poem in this book. I gave it the title
that the reader sees above. If I had included it in this volume, it
would have gone here in this spot.

The main lesson of that piece was:

How dishonest I can be with myself.
This is hard to admit to myself and others.

While I am a person who is perceived
as easily speaking the truth to power,
Of all people, I speak most dishonestly to
It is myself.

In the end, it was about how human and complicated I am. Life is. We all are. I felt relieved to admit that sometimes I am as emotionally fucked up and confused about life as most people are.

A few weeks before finalizing all fifty of the chapters herein, I started to have second thoughts about sharing the poem. It felt harder to share than to write. I was concerned the piece might identify and negatively implicate the persons who were in my life during those hard times. I was trying to be honest as I could be in the poetry, describing scenes and conversations that were deeply hurtful and dysfunctional. I intended to reveal myself, and I did not name any names, yet I feared hurting people if they were ever to read my words. In sobriety, I had learned that I should not make amends to others if it would do them more harm than good, and something of that principle applied here. There was a large swath of unintended consequences that I had not been thinking about until publishing this book drew near.

After much consideration, I decided that this book was not the right platform for sharing my heart on these matters. It felt less like an act of chickening out, and more like an act of care for myself and others. The writing was a defining moment of confession and healing. Even if the choice not to publish it is because it feels too vulnerable right now, that's okay, too. Not everything has to be revealed in this book. There are other ways for me to share my life experience and process about hard choices, bad choices, and how devastatingly good we are at justifying ourselves.

In addition, since I stepped back from publicizing the thing I thought I was most afraid to write about, a whole new set of questions and frameworks for analyzing myself and my situation at that time started coming into clearer view. For that I am grateful.

Because writing about what I thought I was most afraid to write about was so valuable to me, I commend the writing prompt to you. What are you most afraid to write about? Write that thing. Perhaps it will be a chapter in a book of your own.

goodbye, motherhood
5.19.2017

hands hovering near my scalp
I could feel her heat & she mine.
she invoked ancestors, spirit guides & angels.
lying flat front side down, I met her
felt her presence, a pastel pink light near my right foot hovering
cried because I knew that she was she.
all she did was greet me shyly.
I have not met her since, the daughter I never had.

the thought of motherhood left me cold
never felt the warm impulse to bear a child
resented the expectation of it while imagining the likelihood of fulfilling it
the moment I lost her was also somewhat cold, but more like flat
flat-on-back
the presence at my feet less warm, but not at all cold
I cried a little then, and more later.
But I never said goodbye.

now the red flow & silver goodness wanes;
I permanently say goodbye to motherhood.
Wondrous at the manner of her soft, pink arrival
Wondering who she would have become, and the mother I would have been

I never wanted to be a mother
But her soft, pink hello
was the most warm & beautiful greeting a mother ever received.

I Will Not Join
the What The Fuck Army of One
Journal Entry 7.7.2016

I woke up this morning, July 7, 2016
I made tea
I sat in the rocking chair where I say my prayers
       & considered the day ahead
hear my phone in the kitchen 'ting'
indicating a text.
I go make breakfast,
check my phone.
it's a message from Junior
a link to World Star Hip-Hop
Links that Junior sends me from World Star Hip-Hop
are rarely good news.
It was the video.
You ask, "Which video?"
The one the girlfriend took of her fiancée
sitting, shot, next to her, in a car

a cop, still holding a gun on him, on the bleeding man.
There was a four-year-old in the back seat.
THAT video.
& the fact that you have to ask me, "which video?"
WHICH. VIDEO.
WHICH VIDEO in the last TWO DAYS of a black man
being murdered by the police do you mean?
WHICH VIDEO are you referring to?
WHICH VIDEO? the one of Alton Sterling OR
The one of Philando Castile?
WHICH VIDEO did you see this morning?
Well it's so fucked up on so many levels that you have to ask me
WHICH VIDEO
I don't know where to begin.

Usually, where I begin
on a morning like this morning
after watching a video
like that
is with
"WHAT THE FUCK."
WHAT. THE. FUCK.
What the fuck with the cops
What the fuck with "well, not all cops…"
I FUCKING KNOW NOT ALL COPS…
But what the fuck with these white cops
who shoot and kill black people
with NO consequences?

What the Fuck with the word "Bias"?
Was there BIAS? Yes, there was Bias.
Bias – spelled: R-A-C-I-S-M. Racism.
Black people gunned down in their communities.
It's called terrorism.
WHAT THE FUCK.

If I went on, I would never stop writing.

WHAT THE FUCK.

That was my response over two weeks ago
upon waking to the news
of the Orlando Pulse shooting
49 of God's children
most of them queer
most of them Latinx,
lives extinguished while dancing.
WHAT THE FUCK.
What the fuck with religious intolerance?
What the fuck with non-Muslims criticizing Islam?
What the fuck with people criticizing a religion
they know nothing about?
What the fuck with people going to hell
because they don't believe like you do?
What the fuck with Christians, my people,
calling other people terrorists?
Who sanctioned and carried out centuries of terror & murder
against indigenous people of the Americas?
Christians.
Whose Bible justified the slavery of African peoples?
Christians.
Whose theology is the foundation of
homophobia and heterosexism in this country?
Christians.
What the fuck with homosexuality is sin?
What the fuck – get over it already, people.

WHAT THE FUCK with "You have to work within the system."
Why?
What the Fuck is that about?
It's about the system; that's what the fuck that's about.
Man, fuck the system.
What the fuck.
The system.

BUT.
You know what the system fucking loves?
It LOVES What The Fuck rants that lead nowhere.
The system loves

when we blow our tops in private
The system loves isolation.
The system loves individuals.
The system loves white people
Who distance themselves from accountability
& dwell in the comfort of inaction.

I WILL NOT JOIN THE WHAT THE FUCK ARMY OF ONE.

I will not sit in front of screens
& let the totality of my response
to acts of horror be:
WHAT. THE. FUCK.
WHAT THE FUCK.
WHAT THE FUCK with sad & angry face emojis
& hearts & righteous Facebook posts
as the extent of our activity thinking that we're doing something

I WILL NOT ENLIST IN THE WHAT THE FUCK ARMY OF ONE
isolated in the echo chambers of my private rage

I want to be in the WTF Army of Two,
sitting across the table with a cup of coffee
with Celeste
talking
WTF with Lawrence public schools?

I want to be in the WTF Army of Three
with Crescent Moon Healing sisters who understand
there is no healing for any one of us
without healing our communities

I want to be in the WTF Army of Eight
the Guerrilla Society
resisting injustice through articulating truth and love
without judgment

I want to be in the WTF Army of Twelve
with Love Prevails

Disrupting the shit out of my church
& its hate-filled narratives
& practices of violence towards LGBTQ people

I want to be in the WTF Army of 200 people
who came to the #WeAreOrlando vigil
in Lawrence
because we are better together
than we are divided

I want to wake up tomorrow
make my tea
say my prayers
consider my day
check my phone
& not have to say: What The Fuck.

We're going to need an Army to get there.
because it's lonely inside
& dangerous out there.
Will you join me?

Performed at the first-ever LBGTQ Open Mic in Lawrence at El Taller, on the same evening of the day it was written.

From the Hectic
to the Slow Filling of Days
Journal entry 7.31.2017

Why
When
We all know
that the hectic filling
of days
is robbing us of
vital energy
and joy
and slowing
and simplifying
come as
sweet relief
does
the slow filling of days
then seem

as life practice
to be judged
frivolity
when
it is the best
defense
against
our destruction?

The People's Grocery &
the Lynching at the Curve[1]
Original June 2017[2]

In the early spring of 2017, I read a biography of Ida B. Wells-Barnett[3] in preparation for a road trip driving through the South. I intended to connect with the land and graves of my mother's mother's people in eastern Tennessee and continue south to visit some of the well-known sites of the civil rights struggle in Tennessee and Alabama.

---

[1] A short video describing the context of the lynching can be found here: https://lynchingsitesmem.org/news/ida-b-wells-lynching-curve-feature-film-coming-2018.

[2] I completed the final draft of this essay in September 2019. Many thanks to friends and colleagues who contributed to this essay with their honest and corrective feedback, including: Anne Dunlap, Will Green, Andriette Jordan-Fields, Kristina Lizardy-Hajbi, Heike Peckruhn, Nancy Rosas, Brenda Smith White.

[3] *To Tell the Truth Freely: The Life of Ida B. Wells*, Mia Bay (New York: Hill and Wang: 2009). Material specifically on "The Lynching at the Curve" is Chapter 3, pages 82-108.

I'm not entirely sure what prompted me to think Wells' writing was the kind of preparation I needed for the trip. I knew something of her life through shared historical ties to the Methodist Church. I knew her as one of the first African-American women journalists in the United States. I knew she became famous for her detailed reporting on lynching and her anti-lynching lobby campaigns in the late 19th and early 20th centuries. I sensed a need to grasp the history of lynching more thoroughly. It felt relevant to understanding the vitriolic reactions of so many white people to the passionate protests of the #BlackLivesMatter movement that had publicly re-animated the resistance movements of people of color throughout the United States during the previous few years.

From reading Wells, I learned about the People's Grocery and what became known as the lynching at the Curve in Memphis, Tennessee. In 1892, the People's Grocery became the epicenter in Memphis for white economic fear and rage towards black people's economic self-determination. A conflict over a game of marbles escalated. The father of a white boy who lost the game whipped the African-American boy who won the game. W.H. Barrett, the white owner of the grocery store across the street, joined with other white men and attacked a group of black men, who were angered by the beating of the boy. The next day, Barrett led law enforcement to confront the store clerk, which led to another altercation. Barrett then pulled the People's Grocery owners and employees into a legal battle and harassment campaign to undermine this economic competitor in the neighborhood. Barrett stirred up racial fears by spreading a rumor that a white mob planned to attack the store. So the co-owner, the manager, and clerk of the People's Grocery – Thomas Moss, Calvin McDowell, and William Stewart – prepared a defensive, armed stance to protect the property. A confrontation between persons stationed to protect the store and plain-clothed deputies led to gunfire. Along with others, Moss, McDowell, and Stewart were arrested and held without bail. White mobs spent the next three days destroying the Curve neighborhood and the People's Grocery, and Memphis' white newspapers began a smear campaign.

Three days after the shoot-out at the People's Grocery, a white mob descended on the jail. The mob dragged all three men –

Thomas Moss, Calvin McDowell, and William Stewart – out of the jail and lynched them. Throughout the city, a campaign of racial terror by white police officers and white mobs followed the lynching for several days.

At that time, Wells was the first African-American woman co-owner and editor of the Memphis-based African-American newspaper, *The Free Speech*. Already famous for her forthright political analysis of injustice, her editorial on this lynching in *The Free Speech* forced her to relocate from Memphis immediately and permanently due to the threats to her life that resulted from it. This launched her career as a journalist documenting lynching at its height.

The lynching at the Curve was the impetus for Well's exhaustive inquiry into one of the primary white justifications for the atrocity of lynching. Before the events at the People's Grocery, Wells understood the gross generalization that lynching was a justified extralegal response to the threat or accusation of rape that white women attributed to black men. Wells personally knew Thomas Moss, the People's Grocery co-owner, and was close with his family. Wells clearly understood the lynching was a reaction to the economic power of the black community. Afterward, she began her nationwide investigation into the facts surrounding all reported incidents of lynching in 1892. Through extensive travel, research, writing, and speeches, she relentlessly exposed that the prevalent argument for lynching – the defense of the sanctity of white women from the physical violence and sexual predation of black men – was an outright lie.

When I was in downtown Memphis, I found the historical marker dedicated to the memory of Ida B. Wells-Barnett. I decided in the moment to find out where the Curve neighborhood was. I discovered there was another historical marker at the location of the People's Grocery, a few miles away, that I would have to drive to.

I looked carefully for the historical marker on the corner of Mississippi and Walker in Memphis. I was observing the streets as my GPS indicated the increasing closeness of the intersection. I felt my breathing become tighter and my anxiety rising as I drove into the neighborhood. The tangibility of poverty noticeably intensified: dilapidated buildings, boarded-up windows, barbed wire fences, and trash on the streets. My middle-class trained white woman's mind and body felt unsafe. I was disturbed by thinking that my physical response was the result of my racism. I could not disentangle the level of poverty from the fact that all of the people in the neighborhood that I could see were black. Why did I feel this way? My mind and heart caromed between feeling I was succumbing to an old fear and knowing there was nothing to fear in the here and now.

It is important to note that it never dawned on me that my presence in this neighborhood might have been an intrusion fueled by white and class privileges. Though I didn't understand it that way at the time, throughout that trip, I had been engaged in civil rights tourism. At times it was intense and emotional, but there was a sense of distance from the violence about which I was learning. Here at the Curve, I was not at a tourist site. But I had headed out to the corner of Mississippi and Walker as if it were. To take a picture of a sign. A spectator of history. I had drawn on my white privilege to enter the neighborhood and take some photos as though it were a museum. Then I felt uncomfortable and wondered why.

I came to the intersection of Mississippi and Walker. I saw the historical marker for the People's Grocery ahead. I also noticed in my peripheral vision that black men were sitting on the sidewalk against the wall of a store across the street. Their sitting on the ground against the building, as well as the poverty, caused me to think they might be drinking. Were the men sitting across the street from the store drinking or drunk? I do not know. In retrospect, the assumptions I made were racist and classist. I knew nothing about what they were doing there. My internalized racism brought fear-based racist and classist stereotypes to the surface, and that shut me down.

I turned off the car in the parking lot of what is now Sam's Food Market. I felt confused by the forces and feelings moving inside of me. I didn't want to get out of the car. I knew there was no reason to feel threatened, but I did not feel comfortable. My body was feeling anxious and tense. I felt self-conscious. I got out of the car. I did not want to stare at the men, to be a spectator of their existence. But I was also afraid not to look at them, to not acknowledge their presence. I walked towards the historical marker on the sign pole.

The men went quiet for a minute. I went directly to the sign. I took pictures of it with my phone. They realized what I was doing and resumed talking. I never looked at them directly, and I regret this.

I was thirsty, so I went into Sam's Food Market. I was strangely relieved to be greeted by a middle-aged man who appeared South Asian, who, when he saw me, smiled broadly and greeted me with, "Hello, pretty lady." I bought a bottle of water and left. I decided I needed more pictures of the historical marker with the current store sign in the picture. I still felt uneasy. Confused. Why did I feel relieved inside of the store? Because the clerk was not black? Why did I feel ill at ease outside?

This was not the first time I had such a physical acknowledgment of the fear of black men. In one of the first workshops I took on white privilege, the facilitator asked me if I had ever crossed to the other side of the street when a black man approached me. I couldn't remember if I had. Later that same week, in the city where I served as a pastor, walking down the street, I noticed that I physically reacted to a black man walking towards me on the sidewalk. My body inclined to move towards the other side of the street. I had not realized it before. It was a deeply embedded, unconscious reaction. I stayed on the same side of the sidewalk as the man approached me. I remember this as a huge learning about the unconscious levels of actual, physical fear that are a part of the training of white people, and more specifically white women, when it comes to racism in the United States. From this awareness, I was able to examine my fear, work on it, and change my behavior. I was able to see and feel that in all of those circumstances where I reacted in fear, I was never really subjected to any direct threat.

I did not remember this learning when I was at the Curve. Clearly, I felt a potential danger in a space that was not white. It was not that I had never been the only white person in an all-black space before. But the conditions of poverty brought my fear to the surface more acutely. I believe that I found the greeting of the clerk in Sam's Grocery a relief because he was not black. And in this difference, I sensed even more deeply the particularity of white women's racism toward black men, specifically rooted in the context of this awful history of white women, black men, and lynching. A racism that I have inherited as a white woman. A racism that came to the surface in those moments.

Throughout my road trip, I had tried to be conscious of being in my body. I tried to be aware of the real bodies, real violence, real death, and real determination of the people who had lived and struggled in the places I visited.

My ancestors were present in the eastern Tennessee mountains since the days of the Revolutionary War. They had been farmers. Soldiers. What were their relationships with slaves? The Trail of Tears of the Cherokee and other indigenous peoples went right through the lands where they lived. Surely my family had witnessed this? What had they done or not done? I tried to connect with the knowledge of the past in its immediacy in the present. I was not successful in feeling those connections, but I usually stopped to pause and try. I was sadly aware of my lack of knowledge of my own ancestry and history, despite standing at my mother's people's graves. On the corner of Mississippi and Walker, this site of utter white-on-black brutality and black resistance, I found it harder to find the internal space to pause. Yet the bodily connection felt real.

It should not be strange to feel feelings in such a place of violence given what happened there. The fear of poverty and race I experienced at Sam's Food Market was a descendant of the events of the People's Grocery and the lynching at the Curve. I felt sick over the thought that such a tangibly-felt racism and fear of poverty were still that deep within me, but I certainly cannot deny that it was and is now so.

Later reflections on this experience helped me understand that my physical intrusion into the place, my focus on my anxiety, and my mental confusion were a re-centering of my whiteness. I buried my ability to stay curious about the actual neighborhood and the men who were there, to see the layers of my stereotypes about race and poverty, and to consider the lynching itself. I could not get beyond my individual experience in the moment. I have seen this happen so many times in classrooms about identity and difference. White people re-center their own experience, physical discomfort, and difficulty dealing emotionally instead of dealing with the reality of their racism right in front of them. This disables our ability to relate with one another when past and current legacies of harm are felt and grasped. I thought I understood that reaction in myself. Upon further reflection, I feel how the layers of racism and classism continue to peel back to reveal the need for ongoing, critical awareness, and more healing.

Later the same day I went to the Curve, I returned to the rented room where I was staying in another neighborhood in Memphis. I sat on the front porch of the house, sifting through some cedar branches that I had foraged earlier in eastern Tennessee. My presence on the porch attracted two African-American boys riding their bikes up and down the street in the neighborhood. One did all the talking, asking me a series of questions like where I was from and what kind of phone I had. He wanted to know if he could ask a question that might offend me. He asked, "You won't call the cops?" I responded, "Why would I call the cops?" We talked briefly about a few other things. I told him I was about to head inside. Then he asked me a provocative question, which I told him was inappropriate, and I went inside.

That night, as I contemplated the whole day, our interaction haunted me: "You won't call the cops?//Why would I call the cops?" Later I realized he might have thought I went inside and called the cops. A friend with whom I shared this story asked if there were any options other than going inside or calling the cops. Could I have inquired more of him to understand his questions? These inquiries prompted me to see again how unexamined internalized racism deeply limits access to curiosity, creativity, and healing in relationships across racial difference.

"You won't call the cops?//Why would I call the cops?" I would call the cops because that's what white women do. Tell our men. Ask them to protect us. The police are our men. And the posses. And the mobs. Our fathers. Our uncles. Our brothers. This is what happened during lynching. White women called their men. We became the inheritors and the generators of the fear of black men. We have internalized and sowed the anti-blackness taught to us by our families and cultures. By generating the fears and lies, we planted them more deeply within ourselves. These fears and lies continue to perpetuate all forms of violence against black people, whether we are aware of it or not.

At the Curve, I felt the awful embeddedness of those fears and racist stereotypes, and the weight of the grief of continuing to acknowledge this reality as a white woman. The concept of white women's sexual purity was a tool leveraged in defense of white supremacy, by white women themselves. White women evoked in the broader white supremacist culture the fear of black people's freedom through false accusations of black men's violence and silence about the true nature of their relationships with black men. Such accusations and silences are two of the particular ways in which white women have historically enhanced their power.

We intentionally destroyed the lives of black people through appeals to white female innocence, purity and superiority, and black male violence, while simultaneously ignoring and denying that white men have routinely raped black women without consequence.

In the last few years, particularly since the advent of the #BlackLivesMatter movement, I had heard from women of color that their worst relationships with white people were with white women. I heard from white women and saw in our faces the shock and dismay at this news. "We are not these women! Why do you feel this way about us?" There are numerous historical reasons for this. White women need to do our history, search our souls, and hold each other accountable for knowing these reasons. The problems we have honestly relating to one another across differences of race in this country are deeply rooted in white people's unwillingness and inability to deal with the viciousness of our history and to see our racism and classism for what they are. In different ways, places and times, white women have had our own particular role in that history. I saw and felt it within me throughout that day.

The best I could do that day, despite all my education and training, was to allow myself to seesaw between the desire to feel and understand and the desire to deny my feelings and to disengage. I felt powerless, and at the same time, I knew in those situations the power that I – as a white woman – had to act and react in really destructive or truly healing ways. I was ashamed at the vestiges of racism that remained to potentially animate destructive ways and felt guilty that I did not have the resources to enact healing ways. I recognize that I am always on that seesaw, acting in various states of awareness and denial, enacting different levels of harm and healing, every day.

Racism is so pernicious and prevalent within white people in this country, and our denial of it so great, I sometimes wonder if we can heal it. It has become so rooted in our identities as white people I sometimes fear it has become our actual nature. But it is not in our nature. I thank Dr. Edward Antonio, my theology professor at the Iliff School of Theology, for this insight. If we know race to be a social construction created with the intention to divide us upon the lines of economic class, then racism cannot be inherent in any of us. Therefore, it can be deconstructed and healed when we can see ourselves clearly and collectively – and act differently.

In the midst of people-of-color resistance to our white legacy of white racial supremacy and cultural violence, one central component of anti-racist solidarity is to face our cultural and familial training in anti-blackness and the fear of blackness. If we are honest about accepting the deep racism that is at the heart of this nation's existence, then no white person can deny white supremacy's infection at the core of our being. Like any deeply chronic condition, we can't treat it if we are not conscious of its presence, the depth of its infection of our entire system through decades and centuries of built-up racist toxicity in our flesh-and-blood bodies.

White people must face our racist cultural training in order to decode these unfounded fears. We must face them in order to allow for new possibilities to emerge. Confronting ourselves is one way white people can meaningfully move towards our own liberation, as we peel back the layers of what whiteness has done to dehumanize others and dehumanize ourselves. We need to stay open, curious about, and in solidarity with the real differences in our communities and the world. As we do this, we can reach towards freedom and begin to feel and act towards that something new which is possible.

Full Moon Jesus
June 2017

Nothing in my spirituality ever comes as expected, though it is undeniably directed.

The confirmation that I was a Christian came to me practicing Zen meditation at a monastery in Japan during one summer between my years in seminary. My sobriety came to me on an eight-day Jesuit silent retreat, which I did not enter with the thought that I had a drinking problem to conquer. The six-week sabbatical from pastoral ministry I took to deal with the fact that I was an alcoholic introduced me to the chakra system. The chakra system introduced me to my body and the idea that I know things there that I don't know with my mind. Listening to my body while maintaining sobriety introduced me to the reality that I could not sustain pastoral ministry. The church I served at the time introduced me to Marcia, who told me it was obvious the church could not contain me. A Ph.D. program introduced me to Denver. Denver introduced me to herbalism. My herbal teacher introduced me to having a moon sign. Three months in a Carmelite hermitage in a broad, clear-skied southern Colorado valley introduced me to the waxing and waning moon herself.

Two years after returning from Colorado to Lawrence, Massachusetts, I found myself to be some sort of astrology expert. I continued my education in plant medicine – herbalism and essential oils. I also started collaborating with two women who shared a love of spiritual practice in community. We began to offer a ritual on every new moon and every full moon. I incorporated sharing essential oils to connect with the moon energies. Through word of mouth we attracted a few to sometimes twenty persons, mostly young Latinxs. That these gatherings attracted so much interest was astounding.

The ritual we constructed emerged organically. For lack of a better term, I would inadequately describe my sister-collaborators as having an eclectic New Age spirituality. They would open the ritual with an invocation of a pantheon of divine spirits, angels and personages, most of whom I had never heard of.

My primary part, besides the moon talk before the ritual, was to name the directions and the elements. I was surprised how naturally this naming came to me. I had studied the directions and elements briefly in the Celtic-European tradition of my first herbal mentor, but it wasn't something I understood fully. Yet on the first occasion I did this, it was as if I was doing something that I already knew how to do. This had also been my experience of herbalism. When I interacted with plants that I knew nothing about, somehow the interaction invoked something in me that it seemed I already knew, sometime, somewhere. It was an ancient sense. Though at the time the experience of calling on ancestors of anything other than God or the Holy Trinity was more or less foreign to this White, Anglo-Saxon Protestant.

One of our full moon rituals fell on Christmas night. We had been doing the ceremonies regularly for several months, each of the three of us falling into our patterns of conducting the parts of the ritual seamlessly. On the night of the Christmas full moon, we found ourselves in a circle of some dozen kindred. My sisters began their invocations of their many entities. As they were winding down their incantations, it occurred to me that since it was Christmas, it would be good to invoke Jesus and Mary. So very naturally, as they ended their words, I called Jesus and Mary into the circle. This was not my usual part. The energy that descended at that moment was palpable. When I tell this story out loud, I still get goosebumps. I remember some of those present told me afterward how glad they were that I invoked Jesus and Mary to be with us on Christmas. The vast majority of these folx were raised Roman Catholic and evangelical, so Jesus meant something to them.

And Jesus really meant something to me. Almost no one at the time knew that I was an ordained United Methodist minister. Once that knowledge filtered into our community, people sometimes asked me how I bridged my Christian understanding with a practice that most of their families would consider wrong. My simple answer was to appeal to Scripture. God had made the sun, moon, and stars. That we were able to connect to the divine through what God had created would certainly please God's heart.

But the day after the Christmas full moon, I found myself having my own doubts. I felt weird about having called Jesus into the moon circle along with Nematoma, like, whoever that was. Maybe it was wrong. I had been deeply trained that Jesus was not just one among many. Jesus was, well, Jesus. I recognized how deeply I felt held in the notion, and the fear, of "you shall have no other gods before me."

I was engaged with others in ritual who honored and believed in multiple deities, which, intellectually, I would have told you that I affirmed. So I was surprised at the extent to which my own exclusivist thinking gripped me. Why did I think I might be doing something wrong, when neither my cognitive understanding nor my embodied experience of that moment had indicated it was wrong? This recognition led me to understand that I was undoing my own indoctrination.

God had directly intervened in my life in the past to tell me I had a substance abuse problem. My relationship with this God of my understanding since that time had become intimate and personal. So I talked with God: "Like, is this cool with you?" The awakening to my substance abuse had taught me that if I were seriously off track without knowing it, God would intervene.

As Easter approached the following year, I realized that I had not observed the season of Lent at all, which I had done so religiously for twenty years. I decided to go to an outdoor Easter sunrise service with my mom. The Scripture text for the service was from Luke 24:1–12, when women brought spices to the tomb to prepare Jesus' dead body. For the first time, I realized these women were, of course, herbalists. Spices to treat the body. Two figures appear to the women in dazzling clothes and said to them, "Why do you look for the living among the dead? He is not here." I heard a clear message from the text speaking directly to me. "Julie, Jesus is not here. In the church. At all. Julie, Jesus is elsewhere. Julie, why are you looking for him here among what is dead for you. You want him to be here. But he is not here. Your spices are not needed here."

Soon after Easter I was in a book group reading Angela Davis' *Freedom is a Constant Struggle: Ferguson, Palestine, and the Foundations of a Movement.*[1] Davis writes about social movements and the intersections of identity. She describes how there is a fluidity in all things; embrace all the challenges to the boxes we find ourselves in. She points to just how hard it is to truly imagine ourselves into a new world when so many points of difference intersect within and among us. In the deepest ways, we are so ingrained in our ways of relating and understanding the world that we cannot see beyond it. Someone in the reading group said the same was true of our faith in light of Easter, that we were called to "stand inside the truly empty tomb with imagination." Jesus just blew open all of the boxes. Which is how I felt on Easter. The tomb is empty but it is full of possibility. Full moon Jesus. The Christian tradition may be empty for me, but I can stand in the emptiness of it and feel the presence of many more possibilities. The direct interventions of spirit/s moving me beyond all of my confinement have been impinging on my reality for years.

Why is the tradition of monotheism that I have been trained in so limiting? Why does it judge imagining other forms of guidance? Why I asked myself, was I resisting this expansion? As if God and Jesus can't handle that? Like, they gonna be mad? I mean, it's

---

[1] Haymarket Books, 2016.

preposterous. The church, Julie – he is not here. Stand in the empty tomb and imagine.

I can easily recognize that there are deeply personal reasons why it is hard for me to turn from my Christian tradition. I am from generations of Methodists and Methodist preachers. It is a deep part of my family heritage that I do not take for granted. In just about every way – family, education, work – The United Methodist Church has made me who I am. The Christian tradition is the way I found liberation in this lifetime. When anyone asks me what my spiritual tradition or religion is, I say with complete conviction: I am a Christian. Though my own way of expressing my Christian faith has never been the least bit conservative or traditionally evangelical, I can legitimately say that my life was saved through God in Jesus. A personal relationship with God is at the center of my life. Shaking off the old form of this relationship is a process that I do not take lightly.

In addition, I recognize that one reason I resist this transformation is a fear of rejection. In spiritual direction I confessed to myself that I was worried that my experience with Jesus on the full moon and the shift in my spirituality seemed like some froo-froo foolishness, even to me. Full moon Jesus. The silliest thing I ever heard. I was worried what people who have known me for a long time would think of me: a new age white woman. Ugh. I was worried about what I thought of myself. People would think I was no longer a serious, spiritual person. I recognized that these are the kinds of insults hurled at pagans all the time. Then I realized that anyone who really knows me knows damn well how serious I am. Too serious probably, and that one of the consistent messages of my spiritual communication from God is that I seriously need to lighten the fuck up. I mean, this is a God who once got my attention by telling me quite directly that he loved my fuzzy leopard-print slippers. And I was concerned maybe this same God was concerned I was finding meaning and guidance in the cycles of the moon? Monotheism, Julie: Lighten. Up.

It becomes more obvious every day that the church and Christian tradition are no longer what primarily assist me in making space for and imagining this expansive divine. The collective rigidity of form, tradition, and belief contains and constrains the movement of the spirit as it tries to manifest more deeply in my life.

But this movement away from the tradition and theology of Christianity is even deeper than that. When I was in my doctoral program, another student was the first person I knew who identified as a heathen. I didn't know him that well. He was the first person to introduce me to the notion that monotheism is the basis of hierarchy, and hierarchy is the basis of oppression. I already knew from anarchism that hierarchy is the basis of oppression. I hadn't considered that monotheism always has God at the top. No amount of feminist co-creative, process theological argument has ever undone the basic affirmation that God is God and there is no other. "Christ is the head of man, and man is the head of woman, and God is the head of Christ" (1 Corinthians 11:3) was not just a bunch of patriarchal, hierarchical, oppressive bullshit that I had always understood it to be. In this theological hierarchy God is at the top. Full stop. When there is some "One" at the top, there is always some "Bodies" below. This fundamental hierarchy inherent in all monotheistic traditions was a philosophical-theological justification behind every form of contemporary oppression in which Christianity functions as dominant.

In that sense, monotheism is based on God's control extended to the human sphere. My very cursory introduction to paganism, and more deeply to indigenous thinking and living, demonstrated to me that there truly are other ways of understanding the operation of the world that were not hierarchical, or not hierarchical in the same way. Which is why Christianity had to destroy these practices and ways of thinking. Precisely because those traditions had within them a far more diffuse sense of power, which was and is a threat to Christian control.

This collective rigidity of form, tradition, and belief that I experienced personally in the church itself is deeply intertwined with white supremacy and capitalism.

Now again, if you had asked me if I thought Christianity was superior to other religious traditions and practices, I would have told you absolutely and vehemently no. But a ten-week course in which I was placed in a caucus group with other Christians to examine and dismantle our Christian privilege brought this unfortunate supremacy to the surface of my own deeply embedded self-understanding. I have written about this experience elsewhere.[2] I liken it to the same dawning self-awareness of white supremacy that is trained into every white person's soul. This is not judgment; this is description. We cannot escape it, so we had better fucking deal with it.

I also grasp that my own resistance to my self-transformation moving away from the Christian tradition is part of my deeply trained sense that any belief system that moves away from a dominant and dominating monotheism is actually less-than. I hate to admit it to myself and to others, but it is true to my experience.

I can tell that I am still struggling in some moments to let this monotheism go. When I experience a spiritual connection with aspects of creation or supernatural life that are named other than God – the spirits of plants and flowers, the guidance of trees or natural elements, the presence of ancestors or other guides – I am tempted to name this "God-in-all-things." I am attempting to justify that a rose, for example, is actually speaking to me or leading me by saying that is just God speaking through the rose. We pick up this justification throughout the Psalms in the Bible when we declare that the heavens proclaim the glory of God. Indigenous companions have challenged me to consider more deeply the notion that the rose is not speaking for God, but for itself. The rose, the moon, the mountain, the trees – they have their own integrity and they are simply expressing themselves. This does not have to be God, in order that always and forever God still gets to be on top as God, in order for it to be so.

My experience as a lifelong Christian dedicated to social justice arising from my faith in a liberating Christ, and my study of history demonstrates to me time and time again that the thread of violence in Christian supremacy, and white Christian supremacy in particular, has very little to recommend itself any longer as a tradition that primarily redeems. Which is not to say that the Christian tradition does not redeem. Because it did me. It is not that the Christian tradition no longer has this potential for others. But I have

---

[2] See *Confessions of a Christian Supremacist* earlier in this volume.

found that for me the tradition and communal practice is so limiting, and its hierarchy so intricately tied to oppression of every form in this country, that its redeeming capacity can no longer take me forward. Any longer, the history and its attendant theology of domination is too damning and too confining.

I say with the greatest humility and gratitude that a very interventionist personal God inserted their self into my life to save it. Because that was the way in. Which also led to the way out. I remain open to that leading. Currently that undeniable direction is taking me to a much more expansive place of belief and practice – to a Jesus who desires to make their presence known at full moons.

An Existence Hewn of Rock
Journal Entry 2.19.2018

The task to know ourselves
to speak ourselves into existence
an existence hewn of rock
and not sandcastles
is our greatest task
Our inability to focus
to go inside
to the place of knowing & naming
deeply
who we are
and what we want
is as much
on us
as it is
on the forces outside us
that seek our undoing
and even our destruction

because while these forces
are real
so is our capitulation to them
who we think we are
is so easily, is so easily washed away
by the slow creeping of their high tidal insistence
at the edges of our carefully constructed
monuments of sand
that there is almost no hope
of our withstanding
the insistent erasure of our dream
on the constantly creeping & receding shoreline
without a turning within
to shore up the stability
of our foundations

Thank you, church
Journal entry 4.14.2018

Thank you, church
for being the container into which I dropped
my way into my liberation
    a structure for my destiny
    signposts flanked
        teacher-professor
        healer-wounded
        prophet-fighting
        priestess-authority
   you gave me
      family
           education
              community
                 friendship
     work
        retreat
           spirituality
            sobriety
you gave me, fundamentally, God

really, God gave me you
>but ultimately this container
>could not hold me
>and I did not want to be held
and Jesus has offered me his way
>but your way offered increasingly less
>truth & life

i do not know how to properly say goodbye
>with enough humility
>or gratitude equal to my debt to you
so all I can do is to ask you to forgive my debts
and the ways we have trespassed against
>each other

i am your daughter
>both deeply sad
>and incredibly relieved
>that I could not be
>the child of yours
>you expected I would be
but I am forever your legacy
>forever seeking the holiness
>you taught me at the heart
>of life in God
and which I experience as profoundly true.

UnEarthing The Understory
(homage to Lily of the Valley)
5.27.2018

You are elusive
beautiful bells, small & tight
upside-down
you resist capture
giving your best to what lies beneath
veiling the inner parts of your divinity
You, epitome of delicate beauty,
elegance that conceals strength
long single stem supports
slight weight
only flowers & beauty
cause you to bend
what otherwise appears rigid

deep relationship with the forest
pine needles

packed from winter
the broad, soft brown floor from which you emerge,
poke up a pointed, tightly wound green frame
deceiving in your early-stage singularity
you are interconnected to surrounding, sprouting
kindred by the hundreds, thousands
extending your reach over time

Shaded canopy of the white pine
darkish, moist underneath
the place where light peeks
pointed & bright, but briefly
mirroring your essence

slowly broadening green, rubbery leaves like tongues
catch water
dripping down your middle
nourishment funneled precisely to your stem

width contrasts with narrowness,
slightness shoots forth
But all is strength
Softness and Toughness
Weightiness & Lightness both

But
Your Smell,
Your Smell.
Heady crown chakra engagement
fragrance of a million goddesses
intoxicates
A Light that clarifies
& quickly passes
Like the bursting of your flowers.

You only offer yourself fully
if momentarily
to those who care to stop, stoop, speak to you
ask, pull your stem, raise you, smell

The fleeting, shining gift
at the end of a process
months in the dark making

Your fragrance does not waft
bells pointed down
green leaf protectors all around
shroud your exquisite simplicity
decomposing pine receives your best

never let anyone grasp too tightly
anything you have to offer
there is,
you try to demonstrate,
a perfection there
humans are never meant to embody.
only you.

Such Presence.
growth cycle so discreet
But from a carpet of subtlety
bursts a veritable sea of delight
chorus of sisters
swarming the feet of the old, majestic trees
Neither of you, tree nor flower,
more grand than the other

Your root structure,
impossible to see
Not one root, but many
interconnected beneath the forest floor
the power of your connection
may be your greatest strength
the kindred lily who lay all together
in the valley
sharing as one
you do not love to share your patch of ground
& growth with others
your Essence is to spread, to multiply.

You grow less strong and plentiful
in the places where you must compete.

To be on your level
one must get on one's knees and bow
feel your soft, brown pine needle bed;
in this, you bring us to the good earth
while offering us the fragrance of heaven

showing humans
something about learning to grow in ways,
to all appearances
we may not even realize.
the breadth of wonder in all that is coming forth.

Written in Moncrief Sanctuary in Andover, MA, after placing a bowl of water on the forest floor to make a Lily of the Valley flower essence, a kind of plant medicine, when the moon was in the sign of Scorpio. I sat on a tree stump and considered the growth process of the Lily of the Valley that I had observed over the prior month. This piece was created from notes written on that day.

no imposter
Journal Entry 7.9.2018

I can no longer remain within a religious-spiritual tradition that is so limited in its expression of the divine, nor can I reconcile myself to institutional forms & their attendant heteropatriarchal theologies that have destroyed and continue to destroy so many lives. I do this as a matter of my own need for spiritual growth & expansion apart from a container that can no longer hold me, but I also offer it as an act of past & future healing in my lineage of women & all non-conforming people who have been marginalized, wounded, persecuted & killed for speaking & living more expansive truths than the patriarchal church could control or bear. My calling to spiritual leadership in this church was no imposter. Indeed the United Methodist Church was the vehicle for this call, called it out of me, nurtured and formed it. I would be nothing without you.

&
despite how fucked up
something is,

we are addicted
to the familiarity
of that thing. the
comfort of it. The
comfort of not having
to actually change
ourselves
to make that thing
different, to make
ourselves,
different.
the comfort zone
is
the easy way out.
deep transformation
is the narrow path;
the territory of camels
passing through
eyes of needles

&
I'm going to watch the church die
I'm not trying to be melodramatic
All things are in a process of decay,
death.
All things. And need to die.
Most probably, mostly
I'll watch it die to me.

I surrendered my clergy orders in The United Methodist Church on April 4, 2019.

Dust of Stars
Journal Entry 12.22.2018

I am carrying things
weighty things
centuries-old
burdens that are not mine
yet are
      heartache
      destruction
incommensurate
with this lifetime of experience
like they have chosen me
      for my capacity
      to contain
that which one lifetime
is not able to bear
alone

And many lifetimes
          one after a painful other
spill into my
          time-space consciousness
          to pass thru mine
          for healing
And though, or perhaps because
          my this-lifetime burden
          of destruction
                    lives laid waste
          is not so great
They called me – You.
          For Us.
And I do not understand
          who they are
          or why me
          or what healing
and commensurate or not
          their pain passes thru me first
          and then
          their GRATITUDE
It is my own healing also
This healing that I don't even know
that I need
they leave it with me
          in my heart
          and in my cells
Like Gifts
Gifts that will take me
my own lifetime to unwrap
small weighty beautiful boxes
with stars inside them
          the same dust
          of the centuries
          across time
          from which
          they –
          me –
          all were made

This gift
 the container
 arrives full & bursting
 wailing
 a child's hands ripping off paper
 in an instant
 and the thing comes tumbling out
 and then tomorrow
 like it never happened
But the mind ceaselessly
 attempting to smooth
 the crumpled paper
 back out flat
 and straight
 manageable
but it is futile
the contents now
outside the box
can never
be rewrapped
in any way
to fit
neatly
back in
 The mind, he will keep trying
 The heart, who is the container
  will keep denying
  her lover, the mind,
  the ability
  to fit the pieces
   neatly
   back
   into the box
  or to shut the top
   the lid
   at all.
You cannot wrap me back up.
My contents spill, loose
 like water over edges

And there will be crying
             over spilled milk
There is nothing to be ashamed of
             When I have made a mess.
             Leave it on the floor.
             Where it spilled.
             Some things
             Can never be cleaned up
Nothing, but nothing
             like this
             is ever tidy.
Nothing like this.
             This spilling over of the realms
             Another, others
                          into mine
             The mind cannot grasp
             And is not meant to
                          Ultimately
                          in any way
And this, in itself
             Is healing
Letting the heart
             lead the mind
                          to wonder
Only the heart
             could ever
             fully contain
             that which seeks
                          only to be freed, felt
Only the heart
             could ever
             fully welcome
             something so totally unknown & strange
             as completely itself
There is a drowning quality here
             a choking on air & water
             in pain & gratitude
             seeking to be fully expressed
             in a relationship

known at the level
of cells
& spirit
Cells & spirit
& Dust of stars

I wrote this while overcome with the experience of the presence of collective ancestral spirits and gacking out sobs, which had become a feature of my spiritual experience in an occasional but very prominent way during the prior summer. It has occurred to me that the way this presence shows up is not dissimilar to the way many of these writings have come out of me: forceful, unbidden, full of emotion and grace, leaving me grateful and in awe.

When Spires Fall
(Who Are We?)
Honors Convocation
Iliff School of Theology, Denver, CO
4.24.2019

Sacred Text: June Jordan's *Poem for South African Women*
Sacred Music: *We Are The Ones We Have Been Waiting For*
                (Caran Ware Joseph, Daryl Walker, Jenny LaJoye)

When spires fall, who are we?
When spires fall, who are we?
When spires fall,
        be they Gothic, Roman Catholic
        be they white-steepled United Methodist
When spires fall, who are we?
(we are the ones we have been waiting for)

when spires point
        up

to blue skies
clouds filled with daydreaming
of heaven here on earth
radiant light-filled visions
and moonlit skies of night flying
glorious testaments to the divine

when spires point
            up
            to God-forsaken hierarchies
when spires top
            monuments to power
when spires topple
            centuries' tendencies to dominate every landscape
when structures crash
            the ones we claim to resist
            yet we built them
            then they built us
when spires fall, who are we?
(we are the ones we have been waiting for)

over 40 days ago
            some of us proclaimed ourselves
            people of dust and ashes
            proclaiming the rightness of
            returning to earth, right-sized
over a week ago, when we
            peered into the gaping dark gash
            hole at one of the epicenters of
            western christian civilization
The first response was not
            "Let us sit in these ashes."
The first response was
LET US MAKE THE CHURCH GREAT AGAIN.

A mere three days ago, some of us
            peered into the dimly lit cavern,
            a gaping hole of another kind
            ready to encounter the remains of life as we knew it

wanting simply to honor the dead form
of a life that once provided us hope
But there we only found Questions:
"What are you looking for?"
"Why are you looking for the living among the dead?"
"Why are you here?"
HE IS NOT HERE.
When the tomb is empty, who are we?
(we are the ones we have been waiting for)

When spires fall,
when structures we hold dear
come crashing down
and the gaping dark holes contain nothing we expect
and the great wonder of our highest aspirations
mixes with the evils of power & good intention
no sweet distinction between the forms
that lift life up
and the forms that
tear life down
When spires fall, who are we?
(we are the ones we have been waiting for)

I wonder how the trees felt
the cathedral ceiling home to a literal forest of ancient oaks
13,000 trees supporting 210 tons of roof & spire
How relieved were they?
13,000 buttresses turned matchsticks
to relieve themselves of that burden
the weight of centuries of human supremacy
ripped as they had also been
murdered
taken from their land
like millions of others since
by those who decided their bodies
were better served
stripped & exploited for gain
How did those trees feel when they burned?
Did they wail with grief for their children?

Did they cry "Free at last! Free at last!"
Did the trees clap their hands?
Did they shout "Hallelujah!"
with the thousands upon thousands
who had been burned at the stakes
       and hung from
their kindred
Were the ancient oaks glad to finally be released
       their last act to provide a
       massive funeral pyre
       to the reliquaries of domination?
A ritual bonfire around which
       many in the world
       did not mourn
       but celebrated
Like Miriam and the women
       with tambores, dancing, praising:
       "THANK GOD that monuments to destruction
       do not last forever"
and the others who organized well into the night
       around the glowing embers, plotting
"These monuments, if they do not burn to the ground,
       LET US PULL THEM DOWN"

When spires fall, who are we?
(we are the ones we have been waiting for)

The rich and powerful fear nothing more
       than the empty space of pure possibility
       filled with the sounds
       of the pounding of
       thousands of pairs of feet
       of the ones who inspire
       no donations
       whose march began
       with whispers and dreams
and not spires
       but raised fists
       and ferocious self-affirmations

pointing upward
lifting songs & doing drag shows
  the highest amplitude of loving
  the highest altitude of non-conformity
  sparking an uncontrollable heat
  that yes,
    will cause fires
when spires fall, who are we?
(we are the ones we have been waiting for)

Standing in empty tombs,
  What can we imagine?
  Let's not even call it resurrection
  resist the urge to fall back into old habits and concepts
  let's call it creativity
  let's call it joy
  let us call it the threat of possibility
Let us not mock tradition
  but defy convention
Let us not be conformed to this world
  but be transformed by the renewing of our minds
  and our language & our practices
Because
  What if
    the most important things to be said are not sermons
  And what if
    the most important things that need to be written
    are not scholarship
  And what if
    the BEST places to do justice
    are not churches
  and what when
    the most necessary people to lead us to liberation
    are not white
  and what when
    the most life-changing exchanges of meaning
    are not on the internet
And because all of this is already true, what now?

When spires fall, who are we?
(we are the ones we have been waiting for)

When spires fall
        be they Gothic, Roman Catholic
        be they white-steepled United Methodist
when denominations crumble
when broken systems expose our basic vulnerability &
our basic goodness & our basic violence
When the forests are gone
When your scholarship is irrelevant
When your sermon sucks
When the internet crashes
When your position & power are gone
When the climate changes
When Columbine
When Abu Ghraib
When Newtown
When Mother Emmanuel
When Standing Rock
When Yemen
When Berta Caceres
When Palestine
When Tree of Life
When St. Landry Parish
When New Zealand
When Sri Lanka

When all that remains
are ashes &
ceremony &
prayer &
song
When spires fall, who are we?
(we are the ones we have been waiting for)

The week before I gave this address, the Notre Dame Cathedral in Paris, France, burned and its spire fell. That week was Holy Week in the season of Lent for Christians in the Western tradition. The week I delivered this speech, Christians in the West had just celebrated Easter. There are references to the symbols of Lent and Easter throughout the piece, as I delivered it in the United Methodist seminary where I teach. A video of this speech is available at https://youtu.be/IkcWmKaUmsA (go to minute 10).

About Julie

I am a Libra Sun born in the best month of the year in New England, October. As such, I am highly relational, a thinker and over-thinker, a communicator and teacher.

At the time of this publication's release, I live in Lawrence, the absolute best city in Massachusetts.

My primary work is teaching justice and peace studies in all online and hybrid formats for Iliff School of Theology in Denver, Colorado. I'm interested in if and how individual and collective spiritual life and religious traditions and practices are sources of oppression and violence and/or liberation and justice. I am constantly working on what it means to resist and undo systems of hierarchy and domination. I am forever learning and imperfectly embodying what it means to be in solidarity as a white, middle-class person living in a white, settler colonial state bent on destroying the earth and all the earth's human and other-than-human inhabitants.

I met the moon in a Colorado valley desert, and learning its cycles began to change my life, including an ongoing fascination with astrology. I am Leo Moon and Leo Rising, which charts my fundamental desire to express myself in authentic ways.

I journal and practice meditation daily. I am deeply moved by the cultivation and expansion of spiritual life and leadership. I love reflecting on all these things in writing and in person in the communities in which I am a part.

I have spent several years studying plant medicine, which has played a primary role in decolonizing my mind and my religious understanding and practice.

I have a business called *JustJulie*, through which I sell herbal and aromatherapy products and encourage people to treat themselves simply, naturally, and justly. You are welcome to visit at *justjulie.me*.

CPSIA information can be obtained
at www.ICGtesting.com
Printed in the USA
LVHW111330180720
661048LV00002B/372